The SALVATION Book

What does it mean to be a child of God?

By Dave Weeks

The Salvation Book is the incredible story of the Creator of all things and how He communicates His love to every living soul. At a place called Calvary, He gave His only begotten Son, Jesus Christ, to provide salvation to as many who desire deliverance from sin and death. He promised that all who come to Him in faith and a willingness to follow His Word would have everlasting life. All who love light rather than darkness will find Him and become His children.

What does it mean to be a child of God? It is the stories of those who chose to become God's children. It is also the stories of those who loved darkness (evil) rather than good and hated God. They chose to follow the knowledge of evil and become followers of the serpent.

At the beginning of creation, God created two spheres or realms. One was in the heavens, and the other was on earth. He created the heavenly bodies, angels, and many other creatures in the heavens. Lucifer was known as the serpent and the devil. He thought of himself as the highest being in the heavenly realm and had a plan to be the same everywhere else.

On earth, God created humans, non-humans, and all things. He made the first human being in His own image and likeness. Adam was formed from the dust of the earth, and God gave him dominion over His creation. Along with Adam's many work duties, he was given a commandment not to eat of one tree: the tree of the knowledge of good and evil. If he did, he would begin dying until he was dead. Then God created Adam a wife from one of his ribs, and he named her Eve. They begin the story of deliverance from sin and death and are the first to become children of God's eternal kingdom that begins in Revelation 21.

What does it mean to be a child of God?

By

DAVE WEEKS

© 2022

Baptist World Cult Evangelism

P.O. Box 352

Jefferson, GA 30549-0352

www.bwce.org

Unless otherwise specified, all Scripture quotations are taken from the Authorized King James Version.

THE SALVATION BOOK
© 2022 Baptist World Cult Evangelism
P.O. Box 352, Jefferson, GA 30549-0352

Printed by Facing the Facts, Jefferson, GA
Cover by Addyman Design

Printed in the United States of America

All rights reserved. No part of this publication may be reproduced in any manner whatsoever without the publisher's written permission, except for brief quotations in articles and reviews or for use in church Sunday school classes that have met the requirements for approval.

Library of Congress Control Number: 2022906633
Weeks, Dave
The Salvation Book / by Dave Weeks.
p.cm.
Includes bibliographical references
ISBN: 978-0-9910115-6-8 (Paperback)
1. SALVATION THROUGH THE AGES 2. DOCTRINE OF SALVATION. 3. RULES OF INTERPRETATION. 4. MONOTHEISM — ONLY ONE GOD 5. THE TRINITY — ONLY ONE GOD IN THREE PERSONS.

FOREWORD

I could not think of anyone more worthy to write this foreword than the Word Made Flesh, Jesus Christ Himself, the Creator of all things, and the Eternal Son of God.

In the beginning was the Word [Jesus], and the Word was with God, and the Word was God. The same was in the beginning with God. All things were made by him; and without him was not anything made that was made.

And the Word was made flesh, and dwelt among us, and we beheld his glory, the glory as of the only begotten of the Father, full of grace and truth.

And God said, Let us make man in our image, after our likeness: and let them have dominion over the fish of the sea, and over the fowl of the air, and over the cattle, and over all the earth, and over every creeping thing that creepeth upon the earth. So God created man in his own image, in the image of God created he him; male and female created he them.

And she shall bring forth a son, and thou shalt call his name JESUS: for he shall <u>save</u> his people from their sins.

For the Son of man is come to seek and to <u>save</u> that which was lost.

All that the Father giveth me shall come to me; and him that cometh to me I will in no wise cast out. For I came down from heaven, not to do mine own will, but the will of him that sent me. And this is the Father's will which hath sent me, that of all which he hath given me I should lose nothing, but should raise it up again at the last day.

My sheep hear my voice, and I know them, <u>and they follow me</u>: And <u>I give unto them eternal life</u>; and they shall never perish, neither shall any man pluck them out of my hand.

<u>Come unto me</u>, all ye that labour and are heavy laden, and I will give you rest. Take my yoke upon you, and learn of me; for I am meek and lowly in heart: and ye shall find rest unto your souls. For my yoke is easy, and my burden is light.

COMMENTS FROM A FRIEND

It was an honor to be able to read through this book as it was being written. To capture the narrative flow of the Bible concisely is not always an easy task, but Dave Weeks did it masterfully, and you can sense the humility in which he approached the subject of this book. God created us to live with Him, yet when we failed, He never gave up on that original Edenic vision. I pray this book will encourage others as they see just how much God truly loves us.

Mrs. Emily Ertley
Proofreader

What an amazing story it is of love from Genesis to Revelation. *The Salvation Book* will convict AND provide hope. I am so blessed to have a small part in this!

Mrs. Christina Healan
Proofreader

Over the years, I've recorded many how-to books, from home improvement to investing. This book is the first one that has touched me deeper. It's a guide to having everlasting salvation, and Dave Weeks shows you how to receive it correctly. I hope you enjoy listening to it as much as I enjoyed narrating it.

Mark Williams
Narrator

DEDICATION

The silent theme of this text is the Scarlet Thread. It first appeared in the Garden of Eden. Adam and Eve were given a choice to remove their garments of fig leaves for the Sacrificial Garment offered by the LORD God, their Creator. A sinless life was taken to provide atonement for their sin. That was the beginning of the symbolism picturing Jesus Christ, the sinless Lamb of God Who would die for the sins of the world. This poem is dedicated to the Lamb of God, Jesus Christ.

The Scarlet Thread

Picture it red, this Scarlet Thread, the Robe Divine, Who would come in time. Adam and Eve could not fully conceive of Its power, their sins to relieve. This Robe Divine is the Scarlet Thread Who rose from the grave to save the dead. His blood was shed for all mankind and has paid the debt for endless time. The Scarlet Thread was meant for you, but with It, what will you do?

The blood of Jesus Christ His Son cleanseth us from all sin.

Table of Contents

FOREWORD v

COMMENTS FROM A FRIEND vii

DEDICATION viii

    The Scarlet Thread viii

PART ONE — SALVATION STORIES xiv

IN THE BEGINNING 16

GOD KNEW BEFORE 21

LOOKING FOR LOVE 25

THE LOVE CIRCLE 28

THE TWO SEEDS 35

    Two Seeds Misapplied 37

THE AUTHORITY OF SCRIPTURE 43

THE RULES 48

    Ten Figures of Speech 49

ADAM AND EVE 53

CAIN AND ABEL 60

CHILDBEARING 65

SETH AND THE SONS OF GOD 69

   LORD, Lord, lord 70

NOAH'S THREE WORLDS 80

THE GREATEST COMMANDMENT 91

THE BIRTH OF A NATION 95

NOAH'S GREAT-GRANDSON 101

ABRAHAM AT SEVENTY-FIVE 103

ABRAHAM AT EIGHTY-FIVE 118

ABRAHAM AT NINETY-NINE 121

ABRAHAM AT ONE HUNDRED 128

ABRAHAM AT MOUNT MORIAH 133

ABRAHAM'S SERVANT 143

ISAAC, REBEKAH, AND JACOB 147

PART TWO — SALVATION DOCTRINES 155

INTRODUCTION 156

   Three Doctrines of Salvation 158

WHY DO WE NEED SALVATION? 160

Born Of The Spirit 162

Faith 164

Surrender 164

The Wide Gate 165

GENESIS SALVATION 167

Cain And Abel 170

LESSONS FROM GENESIS 175

ROMANS 3 CONTEXT 184

MANKIND'S MORAL COMPASS 189

Love Is A Choice 192

GRACE AND SALVATION 197

FAITH THAT SURRENDERS 199

What Is Faith? 201

Faith And Salvation 202

The Centurion's Faith 204

Faith And Surrender 205

JESUS AND SALVATION 208

The Will Of God And Man 209

Whosoever Will Salvation 211

Sovereign Salvation 213

Elect According To Foreknowledge 216

Blinded Eyes And Hardened Hearts 218

Adoption 220

WORKS SALVATION 222

The Rules 223

ARE YOU A CHILD OF GOD? 225

JESUS' PARTING DAYS 227

Greeks Seek Jesus 229

Washing Of The Feet 229

Many Mansions 230

Vine And Branches 230

The Holy Spirit 231

Lovest Thou Me? 232

The Kingdom of Israel 233

The Kingdom Of God 234

PART ONE — SALVATION STORIES

IN THE BEGINNING

In the beginning God created the heaven and the earth (Genesis 1:1).

In the beginning, when God created all things, He created two realms. One realm or sphere was heavenly (all the heavens), and the other was earthly (our planet earth). He created different kinds of beings in both of these places.

The LORD (*Yahweh*/Jehovah) God gave His creatures different positions, duties, and power. In the heavenly realm, God created many kinds of heavenly beings: angels, cherubims, seraphims, and other living creatures.

He also created many kinds of earthly beings: animals, birds, fish, everything that creeps, and above all other beings, man and woman. When God created Adam, He made him in His own image and likeness. What image and likeness was that? It was the image and likeness of God's only begotten Son: Jesus Christ, the Eternal Son of God. The LORD gave Adam a mind to think and reason, a pure and sinless soul, and the free will to choose to love and obey Him. Without the free will to choose, love would have no value to God or anyone else. The LORD made Adam a helpmate, Eve, to love, cherish and bring forth children to fill the earth. At the end of Genesis 1:31, God said this about what He had created: *And God saw every thing that he had made, and, behold, <u>it was very good</u>. And the evening and the morning were the sixth day.* Then something bad happened that changed this *very good* in both realms.

One of God's heavenly creatures was filled with pride and thought himself able to rise above his Creator. He was the first creature to sin. He is called the serpent in Genesis 3:1, then a long list of names identifies him with evil and wickedness. Some of the names appear as figures of speech for kings and places, but they all have one thing in common: he is a liar, murderer, and God-hater. He is called the king of Tyre, Lucifer, the anointed cherub, the king of Babylon, Satan, the great dragon, the devil, the god of this world (meaning the god of the wicked). The serpent has many other names, but he is not worthy of the space to list them.

The Children of God

The remarkable and wonderful story of salvation existed in the mind of God, our Heavenly Father, our Blessed Savior, and the Holy Spirit before *ever* the world began. "Creation ended" by God saying it was *finished* in Genesis 2:1, *Thus the heavens and the earth were finished, and all the host of them.* [God, Who is infinite in knowledge, foresight, and all things, everything, all the events that did and will happen, He knew it both before and after the above verse was written.] In Revelation 21, God will have created a new heaven and new earth. Our present earth, sea, and its heavenly atmosphere will be destroyed. Then a new earth and heaven above will be created. The children of God will abide there eternally with our Savior, Jesus Christ.

From Scripture, how do we know that Adam and Eve were born again or, better said, born of the Spirit? We know from Jesus' dialogue with Nicodemus. Jesus told him no one would see or enter the kingdom of God without being born of the Spirit.

What happens next when a person is born of God? That person becomes a part of the Body of Christ as stated in 1 Corinthians 12:13-14, *For by one Spirit are we all baptized into one body, whether we be Jews or Gentiles, whether we be bond or free; and have been all made to drink into one Spirit. 14 For the body is not one member, but many.*

The Lamb's book of life records all the names of those entering the kingdom in Rev. 21. Children of God are also called children of the kingdom in Matthew 13:38, *The field is the world; the good seed are the <u>children of the kingdom</u>; but the tares are the <u>children of the wicked one</u>.* The two seeds continue until Rev. 21, then, there is only one, and they are the children of the kingdom.

As the LORD finished questioning Adam and Eve, He spoke to the serpent. Scripture describes a long battle: warfare between the serpent and God. The serpent thought he had reached his position of power and was about to take his place on the throne as the god of this

world. Then the LORD God said this to him in Genesis 3:15, *And I will put enmity between thee and the woman, and between thy seed and her seed; <u>it shall bruise thy head</u>, and thou shalt bruise his heel.* Adam and Eve would soon leave Eden, no longer created beings broken by sin, but as children of God and children of His eternal kingdom of righteousness by God's grace, repentance, and faith in the Sacrificial Garments they wore. Putting on those garments was picturing salvation in Jesus Christ. Genesis begins enmity between the two seeds with Cain and Abel. Abel gave his life to Christ at salvation, and for him to die was gain. The serpent is called a liar and murderer by Christ in John 8:44, *Ye are of your father the devil .... He was a murderer from the beginning, and abode not in the truth, ... When he speaketh a lie, he speaketh of his own: for he is a liar, and the father of it.*
The salvation story has a Scarlet Thread which is the blood of Christ, the Lamb of God. He gave His life for you. Will you surrender your life to Him now?

GOD KNEW BEFORE

But Jesus did not commit himself unto them, because he knew all men. And needed not that any should testify of man: for he knew what was in man (John 2:24-25).

Do you remember reading through the New Testament numerous times and coming across verses like these?

Matthew 9:3-4

And, behold, certain of the scribes said within themselves, This man blasphemeth. And Jesus knowing their thoughts, said, Wherefore think ye evil in your hearts?

Mark 2:8

And immediately when Jesus perceived in his spirit that they so reasoned within themselves, he said unto them, Why reason ye these things in your hearts?

Luke 6:8

But he [Jesus] knew their thoughts and said to the man which had the withered hand, Rise up, and stand forth in the midst. And he arose and stood forth.

Yes, Jesus knew men's thoughts before they were ever spoken. God knows everything about each of us. Jesus knows how many hairs one's head has. Not only does Jesus know mankind, He knows all of His creation. The Lord knows the number of the stars and gives each one a name. His understanding is infinite as recorded in Psalms 147:4-5 *He telleth the number of the stars; he calleth them all by their names. 5 Great is our Lord, and of great power: his understanding* [intelligence] *is infinite* [impossible to measure.]

So, let's connect the dots of God's infinite knowledge, understanding, and wisdom to a verse telling us what He knew about salvation before He created anything in the beginning. If you can grasp the truth in this verse, you will know that God knew who would be saved and who would be lost from the foundation of the world. Revelation 13:8, *And all that dwell upon the earth shall worship him* [the beast, the antichrist]*, whose names are not written in the book of life of the Lamb slain from the foundation of the world.* Revelation 20:15 *And whosoever was not found written in the book of life was* *cast into the lake of fire.*

God knew, before the world was created, who would receive the Sacrifice of His Son and who would not. God knew the *whosoever* and *as many* people because of His infinite foreknowledge. This group He called *the elect according to His foreknowledge.* Why were they called the elect or His chosen? Because they of a free will and in a good and honest heart chose Him by their faith in His Word. Mark 8:34-36 *And when he had called the people unto him with his disciples also, he said unto them,* <u>Whosoever will</u> [whosoever will people vs. the whosoever won't people] *come after me, let him deny himself, and take up his cross, and follow me. 35 For* <u>whosoever will</u> *save his life* [the whosoever won't people] *shall lose it; but* <u>whosoever shall lose his life for my sake and the gospel's</u>, *the same shall save it. 36 For what shall it profit a man, if he shall gain the whole world, and lose his own soul?* Luke 8:15, *But that on the good ground are they,* <u>which in an honest and good heart</u>, *having* <u>heard the word, keep it</u>, *and bring forth fruit with patience.* 1 Peter 1:2 *Elect according to the foreknowledge of God the Father, through sanctification of the Spirit* [born of the Spirit], *unto obedience and sprinkling of the blood of Jesus Christ: Grace unto you, and peace, be multiplied.* What did God do for those who chose Him? He predestinated them to be conformed to the image of His dear Son and, through adoption (which is positional rather than relational), immediately made them heirs to the inheritance of His Son, Jesus Christ. Here's how that is said in Romans 8:29, *For whom he did foreknow, he also did predestinate to be conformed to the image of his Son, that he might be the firstborn among many brethren.* The *as many* and *whosoever will* come to Christ by their faith in God's Word and with a surrendered life. Salvation is God's story of victory for those who bowed at the Savior's cross and are washed in His precious blood.

Jesus, we love You and long to be like You and be with You. Even so, Lord Jesus, come!

LOOKING FOR LOVE

Herein is love, not that we loved God, but that he loved us, and sent his Son to be the propitiation for our sins (1 John 4:10).

Did you ever wonder as you read through Genesis where love begins? What do I mean by that? Well, think about God walking in the garden in the cool of the day with Adam and how their relationship begins to develop. How does God, the Creator, Lord (we would say Boss), and Lawgiver become Someone we love? How does one get to the place in life when they can say what this verse says in Matthew 22:37? *Jesus said unto him, Thou shalt love the Lord thy God with all thy heart, and with all thy soul, and with all thy mind.* Why does God have to give us a commandment to love Him? Where do you find the answers to these questions?

The answer is clear from the beginning: We know that God, the One Triune God Who is Three Eternal Persons, Father, Son, and Spirit, first loved us. How does a child of God feel that love? His love is felt by His presence, voice, words, and deeds. All of this was first experienced by Adam, Eve, and their first two sons, Cain and Abel. But in order for love to be valuable, it must be a choice. God made His choice to love mankind before the world ever began, as is mentioned in Revelation 13:8, *And all that dwell upon the earth shall worship him, whose names are not written in the book of life of the Lamb slain <u>from the foundation of the world</u>.* In the mind of God, Jesus was slain before the world was created. For this to be true, our Lord's human body also existed. It was Jesus Who walked in the garden with Adam and Eve. He appeared to them in human form, a bodily form like unto the Son of Man.

Love began with God Himself; for God is love, perfect love. 1 John 4:8 *He that loveth not knoweth not God; for <u>God is love</u>.* The Father, Son, and Spirit love each other perfectly. They created mankind to love and for us to love Him. The reason people don't love God is because they don't know Him. They have never been born of His Spirit. They exist in many religious forms, yet they do not have the Holy Spirit dwelling within them. Here this is explained as the love factor in 1 John 5:1-3, *Whosoever believeth that Jesus is the Christ is born of God: and every one that loveth him* [the Father] *that begat loveth him* [the Father's children] *also that is begotten of him* [the Father]. *2 By this we know that we love the children of God, when we love God, and keep his commandments. 3 For this is the love of God* [obedience generated by our love for Him], *that we keep his commandments: and his commandments are not grievous* [difficult to obey because we love Him].

Love's beginning has no beginning, for it is as eternal as God Himself. He is love and created mankind as objects of His love. When Jesus presented the garments to Adam and Eve, He was presenting Himself as the gospel of His love for His creation. For love to be valuable to God, it had to be mankind's choice. It is His love that is asking you to believe He is the Son of God and that you would surrender your life to Him. Will you do that right now? It's your choice, right?

THE LOVE CIRCLE

Jesus wept. Then said the Jews, Behold how he loved him (John 11:35-36)!

The previous chapter's text would not be complete without the wonder of these three people: Mary, Martha, and Lazarus. Seemingly out of nowhere, they appear. Jesus is the One who completes this love circle. Now, the Son of God is the Son of Man. Until our Lord's incarnation, He appeared as a person in human form. Now through His virgin birth, He is God manifest in the flesh.

Mary, Martha, and Lazarus give us a preview of the reality of faith in Jesus Christ in the human realm. How Jesus felt about them and how they felt about Him is what being a child of God is. God left out the details of how this relationship began, but as believers, we know it never ended. We learn from this wonderful story that such love and friendship can and does exist with God and His children.

When Jesus returns to Bethany, Lazarus is dead. Both

Martha and Mary have a conversation with Jesus before He raises Lazarus from the dead. These conversations place deep feelings of sorrow and pain in our hearts as we read them. One can almost sense the anger Jesus must have at this moment for the serpent, for it was his lying tongue that beguiled Eve and led her and Adam to suffer the loss of innocence and all mankind to suffer the pains of death. These verses have some genuine expressions of passion, and we see them as we read in John 11:20-28:

20 Then Martha, as soon as she heard that Jesus was coming, went and met him: but Mary sat still in the house.

21 Then <u>said Martha</u> unto Jesus, Lord, <u>if thou hadst been here, my brother had not died.</u>

[Why weren't you here, Jesus?]

22 But I know, that even now, whatsoever thou wilt ask of God, God will give it thee.

[Martha is a person of great faith in God and Jesus.]

23 Jesus saith unto her, Thy brother shall rise again.

24 Martha saith unto him, I know that he shall rise

again in the resurrection at the last day.

[Martha believed God's Word.]

25 Jesus said unto her, I am the resurrection, and the life: he that believeth in me, though he were dead, yet shall he live:

[Jesus will increase her faith.]

26 And whosoever liveth and believeth in me shall never die. Believest thou this?

[Jesus gives the "*never-die*" question.]

27 She saith unto him, Yea, Lord: I believe that thou art the Christ, the Son of God, which should come into the world.

[Martha is still troubled that her brother is dead.]

28 And when she had so said, she went her way, and called Mary her sister secretly, saying, The Master is come, and calleth for thee.

This leaves us with a question. What question is that? If we are saved, do we believe that we will never die? Yes, or no? Never means never, so what is Jesus talking about when He says saints will never die? If we understand that death means separation, Jesus' "never die" question becomes clear. There are three kinds of death or separation. Spiritual death, which is separation from God because of sin. Physical death which is the separation of soul and spirit from the body. And eternal death, which is eternal separation from God in the lake of fire. The moment a person is saved, the Spirit of God gives them eternal life and indwells that person. The Holy Spirit indwells us and is our source of life forever: John 14:15-17, *If ye love me, keep my commandments. 16 And I will pray the Father, and he shall give you another Comforter, that he* [the Holy Spirit] *may <u>abide with you for ever</u>; 17 Even the Spirit of truth; whom the world cannot receive, because it seeth him not, neither knoweth him: but ye know him; <u>for he dwelleth with you, and shall be in you.</u>*

Mary's meeting with Jesus follows and is recorded here in John 11:32, *Then when Mary was come where Jesus was, and saw him, she fell down at his feet, saying unto him, <u>Lord, if thou hadst been here, my brother had not died.</u>* [Mary was sobbing and heartbroken, because Jesus was not there when her brother died.] The following verses show our Lord's great love and deep sorrow and His groaning with anger in the pains of death gripping His beloved friends. Death was the result of the serpent deceiving Eve in the garden. John 11:33-36, *When Jesus therefore saw her weeping, and the Jews also weeping which came with her, he groaned* [with anger] *in the spirit, and was troubled, 34 And said, Where have ye laid him? They said unto him, Lord, come and see. 35 Jesus wept* [He wept with them.]. *36 Then said the Jews, Behold how he loved him!*

There is only one more verse to this story, and it keeps being retold throughout the ages. Mary, Martha, Lazarus, and the disciples are all together with Jesus, and Mary comes forth and honors her Lord with great love and anoints His feet. What a moment this is for all but Judas Iscariot. In a few days, the Lamb of God will become the Sacrifice for the sins of all people. Here's that great moment that Jesus commanded to be remembered wherever the gospel is preached in the world. John 12:1-7, *Then Jesus six days before the passover came to Bethany, where Lazarus was which had been dead, whom he raised from the dead. 2 There they made him a supper; and Martha served: but Lazarus was one of them that sat at the table with him. 3 Then took Mary a pound of ointment of spikenard, very costly, and anointed the feet of Jesus, and wiped his feet with her hair: and the house was filled with the odour of the ointment. 4 Then saith one of his disciples, Judas Iscariot, Simon's son, which should betray him, 5 Why was not this ointment sold for three hundred pence, and given to the poor? 6 This he said, not that he cared for the poor; but because he was a thief, and had the bag, and bare what was put therein. 7 Then said Jesus, Let her alone: against the day of my burying hath she kept this.* Mary knew this.

Let's look at how tears, death, sorrow, crying, and pain are ended as Jesus calls Lazarus back to life after four days in the grave. The joy they all felt is the promise of these kingdom verses in Revelation 21:1-5:

1 And I saw a new heaven and a new earth: for the first heaven and the first earth were passed away; and there was no more sea.

2 And I John saw the <u>*holy city, new Jerusalem*</u>*, coming down from God out of heaven, prepared* <u>*as a bride*</u> [a <u>simile</u> describing the beauty of the city] *adorned for her husband.*

3 And I heard a great voice out of heaven saying, Behold, the tabernacle [dwelling place] *of God is with men* [forever]*, and he* [Jesus our Savior] *will dwell with them* [the kingdom children, the good seed of Matt. 13:38]*, and they shall be his people, and God himself shall be with them, and be their God.*

4 And God shall wipe away all <u>*tears*</u> *from their eyes; and there shall be no more* <u>*death*</u>*, neither* <u>*sorrow*</u>*, nor* <u>*crying*</u>*, neither shall there be any more* <u>*pain*</u>*: for the former things are passed away.*

5 And he that sat upon the throne said, Behold, I make all things new.

Thank You, Lord, for so great a salvation and the truth that a child of God will *never die.* And for giving us the Comforter, the Holy Spirit, Who abides with us forever. Thanks for loving us as only You can.

THE TWO SEEDS

And I will put enmity between thee and the woman, and between <u>thy seed</u> and <u>her seed</u>; it shall bruise thy head, and thou shalt bruise his heel (Genesis 3:15).

The story of salvation is the division between two seeds. They are the seed of the serpent and the seed of the woman. The serpent's seed is the devil who became wicked and sinned because of his pride. He is the father of sin. The seed of the woman is Christ. He is the Creator of all things and the Eternal Son of God. The Father made Him to be sin for us, *who knew no sin; that we might be made the righteousness of God in Him.*

The two seeds divide the <u>world</u> into two people groups. As you read the Scriptures, identifying these people groups enables the reader to apply the context correctly. When people groups are not recognized, the application of a text may appear to reference two groups instead of only one group. Often this is the case as a speaker takes this passage from Jeremiah 17:9 *The heart* [Whose heart?] *is deceitful above all things, and desperately wicked: who can know it?* Is this verse speaking about both people groups or just one? Just one, the seed of the serpent. An incorrect application is a result of not correctly identifying the group.

As you read through your Bible, you should learn to recognize these two seeds. Psalms 1:1-6 is an excellent place to begin developing your consciousness of the two seeds.

Psalms 1:1-6   The two seeds are underlined.

1 Blessed is the <u>man that walketh not</u> in the counsel of the <u>ungodly</u>, nor standeth in the way of <u>sinners</u>, nor sitteth in the seat of the <u>scornful</u>.

2 But <u>his delight is in the law of the LORD</u>; and in his law doth he meditate day and night.

3 And he shall be like a tree planted by the rivers of water, that bringeth forth his fruit in his season; his leaf also shall not wither; and whatsoever he doeth shall prosper. [Note: vs. two and three, seed of the woman]

4 The <u>ungodly</u> are not so: but are like the chaff which *the wind driveth away.*

5 Therefore the <u>ungodly</u> shall not stand in the judgment, nor <u>sinners</u> in the congregation of the <u>righteous</u>.

6 For the LORD knoweth the way of the <u>righteous</u>: but the way of the <u>ungodly</u> shall perish.

Two Seeds Misapplied

Perhaps the most common error of not identifying the two seeds is found in Romans 3:10-18. What people commonly miss is *As it is written.* What follows is a quote from Psalms 14:1-6 describing the seed of the serpent (the wicked) as they persecute the seed of the woman (the righteous or the saved). *As it is written* [in Psalms 14 and 56], *There is none righteous, no, not one: 11 There is none that understandeth, there is none that seeketh after God. 12 They are all gone out of the way, they are together become unprofitable; there is none that doeth good, no, not one. 13 Their throat is an open sepulchre; with their tongues they have used deceit; the poison of asps is under their lips: 14 Whose mouth is full of cursing and bitterness: 15 Their feet are swift to shed blood: 16 Destruction and misery are in their ways: 17 And the way of peace have they not known: 18 There is no fear of God before their eyes.*

The Romans passage is most often quoted by those who have no idea of its context in the Psalms. When the two seeds (the wicked, the God-haters, and the righteous, those who are God's children) are not recognized and identified, the verses are made to represent all people instead of just the wicked. The unfortunate result of this error is the false doctrine of **total depravity.** What is that? It is the doctrine that teaches that all humans have no moral compass after the fall. As a result, they always choose evil rather than good. Adam and Eve proved that to be false when they put on the garments of fig leaves. They could have just enjoyed the lust of the flesh and done nothing. They chose to cover themselves instead. All people know both good and evil and have a moral compass, but some choose darkness rather than light because the darkness is what they love. John 3:19-20, *And this is the condemnation, that light is come into the world, and* <u>*men loved*</u>

<u>darkness rather than light,</u> *because their deeds were evil. 20 For every one that doeth evil hateth the light, neither cometh to the light, lest his deeds should be reproved.*

Recognizing this error is easy to see by observing the first and most important interpretation rule, the context rule. Please look at the verses in Romans from their context *as it is written* in Psalms 14 and 53.

Rom 3:10-18

10 As it is written, There is none righteous [of the wicked], *no, not one:*

11 There is <u>none</u> that understandeth, there is none that seeketh after God.

12 They are <u>all</u> gone out of the way, they are together become unprofitable; there is <u>none</u> that doeth good, no, not one.

13 Their throat is an open sepulchre; with their tongues they have used deceit; the poison of asps is under their lips:

14 Whose mouth is full of cursing and bitterness:

15 Their feet are swift to shed blood:

16 Destruction and misery are in their ways:

17 And the way of peace have they not known:

18 There is no fear of God before their eyes.

Psalms 14:1-6

1 The fool [the wicked] *hath said in his heart, <u>There is no God</u>. They* [the wicked] *are corrupt, they* [the wicked] *have done abominable works, there is none* [the wicked] *that doeth good.*

2 The LORD looked down from heaven upon the children of men [the wicked], *to see if there were any that did understand, and seek God.*

3 They [the wicked] *are all gone aside, they are all together become filthy: there is none* [the wicked] *that doeth good, no, not one.*

4 Have all the workers of iniquity [the wicked] *no knowledge? who eat up **my people*** [the children of God] *as they eat bread, and call not upon the LORD.*

5 There were they in great fear: for God is in the generation of the righteous [the children of God].

6 Ye have shamed the counsel of the poor [the children of God], *because the LORD is his refuge.*

The Lord gave His disciples a parable to help them see the two seeds and what they represent in Matthew 13:36-40, *Then Jesus sent the multitude away, and went into the house: and his disciples came unto him, saying, Declare unto us the <u>parable of the tares</u> of the field. 37 He answered and said unto them, He that soweth the good seed is the Son of man; 38 The field is the world; <u>the good seed are the children of the kingdom</u>; but <u>the tares are the children of the wicked one</u>; 39 <u>The enemy that sowed them is the devil</u>; the harvest is the end of the world; and the reapers are the angels. 40 As therefore the tares are gathered and burned in the fire; so shall it be in the end of this world.* Learning to recognize the two seeds will give you peace of mind knowing that people choose their course in life. God made salvation possible for everyone. But God, in His infinite foreknowledge, knew who would say yes and who would say no to the gift of salvation. Christ became sin for the world, meaning every soul as written here in 2 Peter 2:1, *But there were false prophets also among the people, even as there shall be* *false teachers among you, who privily shall bring in damnable heresies, <u>even denying the Lord</u> **that bought them**, and bring upon themselves swift destruction.*

Yes, Christ even died for those who denied Him. He shed His blood for all, not just the saved. If anyone teaches differently, he has this verse and many others to reprove him. This is one test of the authority of Scripture or the authority of false teachers.

I think that John 3:16 is an appropriate way to close this chapter with God smiling and adding His blessing, don't you? If you really want the truth, Truth is speaking to you. Please listen!

John 3:16 *For <u>God so loved the world</u>, that he gave his only begotten Son, that whosoever believeth in him should not perish, but have everlasting life.*

THE AUTHORITY OF SCRIPTURE

Jesus answered and said unto them [the Sadducees], Ye do err, not knowing the scriptures, nor the power of God (Matthew 22:29).

Why did I start the *Salvation Book* by explaining the rules that guard the authority of Scripture? The reason is because of Genesis 3:1-5, where the serpent took a verse of Scripture and changed the interpretation from literal to figurative. Take a look and see what he did: Genesis 2:16 *And the LORD God commanded the man, saying, Of every tree of the garden thou mayest freely eat: 17 But of the tree of the knowledge of good and evil, thou shalt not eat of it: for in the day that thou eatest thereof thou shalt surely* [most certainly] *die.*
So, what would most certainly happen if they ate from that tree? They would die! What did the lying, deceiving serpent (the devil) say? Genesis 3:4-5, *And the serpent said unto the woman, <u>Ye shall not surely die</u>: 5 For God doth know that in the day ye eat thereof, then your eyes shall be opened, and ye shall be as gods,*

knowing good and evil. This is the change from literal to figurative. The devil said you wouldn't die; you would get more knowledge. He changed the meaning of the verse from literal to a figure of speech called an allegory. What's that? It is a picture, poem, or story that can be interpreted to have a hidden meaning. From this time on, the devil knew that a lie was as good as the truth if you could get someone to believe it. And his wicked scheme has been working ever since. Jesus made these remarks about the lying devil who appeared as a serpent to Eve in John 8:44, *Ye* [the unbelieving Jews] *are of your father the devil, and the lusts of your father ye will do. He was a murderer from the beginning, and abode not in the truth, because there is no truth in him. When he speaketh a lie, he speaketh of his own: for he is a liar, and the father of it.*

In the following chapter, we will see how the authority of Scripture was challenged and how its authority was lost and regained. There is an ongoing battle between good versus evil and right and wrong, but we know God's children have the final victory.

So, how does God protect the authority of His Word? He gave us some good examples in Matthew. Jesus showed the Sadducees that their denial of the resurrection violated the <u>harmony rule</u>. <u>What's the harmony rule</u>? It says that no truth in Scripture will ever contradict itself. Jesus applied this rule by quoting Matthew 22:31-32, *But as touching the resurrection of the dead, have ye not read that which was spoken unto you by God, saying, 32 I am the God of Abraham, and the God of Isaac, and the God of Jacob? God is not <u>the God of the</u> dead, but of the <u>living</u>*. Jesus corrected the interpretation of the Sadducees by showing them God is the God of the living. Abraham, Isaac, and Jacob were alive and would be like the angels at their resurrection. When Jesus was resurrected, Old Testament saints were also resurrected: Matthew 27:50-53 *Jesus, when he had cried again with a loud voice, yielded up the ghost. 51 And, behold, the veil of the temple was rent in twain from the top to the bottom; and the earth did quake, and the rocks rent; 52 And the graves were opened; and many bodies of the saints* *which slept arose, 53 <u>And came out of the graves after his resurrection, and went into the holy city, and appeared unto many.</u>*

Jesus corrected the Pharisees by asking them a question that demanded that the context's authority be applied. It was a well-known verse to religious leaders, but they would not acknowledge its revealed truth. The same is true of many people today. This example is the most compelling application of rule number one, the context rule. Take a look at Matthew 22:41-46, *While the Pharisees were gathered together, Jesus asked them, 42 Saying, What think ye of Christ? whose son is he? They say unto him, The Son of David. 43 He saith unto them, How then doth David in spirit call him Lord, saying, 44 The LORD said unto my Lord, Sit thou on my right hand, till I make thine enemies thy footstool? 45 If David then call him Lord, how is he his son? 46 And no man was able to answer him a word, neither durst any man from that day forth ask him any more questions.*

Jesus quoted Psalms 110:1, *The LORD* [Father] *said*

unto my Lord [the Messiah, His Son], *Sit thou at my right hand, until I make thine enemies thy footstool.* Then Jesus asked the Pharisees if David called his son Lord [meaning He is God], how is He his Son? This verse teaches both the humanity and the deity of the Messiah, the Lord Jesus Christ; God manifests in the flesh, whom the Jewish leaders rejected.

The context and harmony rules are the two most essential watch guards of Scripture. They protect the authority of God's Word by exposing those who ignore them. The rules guard the truth and expose error.

The Berean Principle

Acts 17:11
"... they received the word with all <u>readiness</u> of mind, and searched the scriptures daily, whether those things were so."

THE RULES

Study to show thyself approved unto God, a workman that needeth not to be ashamed, rightly dividing the word of truth (2 Timothy 2:15).

Here are the rules which guard any author's authority in written text, especially the Word of God. When Jesus corrected the misinterpretations of the religious leaders of His day, He did so by applying these rules. Learning to recognize them when reading your Bible will keep you from making Eve's same mistake. You will know the difference between what God said and the devil's lies. Is it that simple? Yes, it is. Any truth in Scripture will never contradict itself. You will see that!

1. Context Rule – The weaving together of words in phrases, sentences, paragraphs, chapters, or the entire Bible, which <u>can shed light on</u> and <u>adds to its meaning</u> in a passage, i.e., Rom. 3:10-18; Gen. 3:15; Psa. 14;53.

2. Harmony Rule – It is the law of no contradiction. A truth that is God-given will always be in harmony with

the whole of God's Word, i.e., Genesis 3:21, *Unto Adam also and to his wife did the LORD God make coats of skins and clothed them.* 2 Pet. 2:1; 1 Joh. 2:2; 1 Tim. 2:1-4

3. Language Rule – The awareness of which language is being used in verse, i.e., literal, figurative, or symbolic, and the grammatical functions that apply to each part of speech. John 8:58 Jesus said, *Before Abraham was, I am.* John 10:9 *I am the door...* Rev. 8:6 *And the seven angels which had the seven trumpets prepared themselves to sound.* The trumpet is a symbol of judgment. See "Ten Figures of Speech."

4. Grammar Rule – Recognizing and agreeing with gender and other grammatical rules that govern its interpretation, i.e., Eph. 2:8; 1Cor. 12:4-9

Ten Figures of Speech

al-le-go-ry n., pl. **al-le-go-ries**. **1.** A picture, poem, or story that can be interpreted to have a hidden meaning. Gen. 3:4-5; Gal. 4; Isa. 5; and Matt. 12:43:45 are examples of allegories.

an-thro-po-mor-phism n. A figure of speech that

attributes human motivation, characteristics, or behavior to God. Ps.91:4, *He shall cover thee with his feathers, and under his wings shalt thou trust: his truth shall be thy shield and buckler.*

eu-phe-mism n. The act or an example of substituting a mild, indirect, or vague term for one considered harsh, blunt, or offensive: Example: "asleep" in 1 Thess. 4:15

hy-per-bo-le n. A figure of speech in which exaggeration is used for emphasis or effect, as in *"I could sleep for a year,"* or *"This book weighs a ton."* Matt. 19:*24 And again I say unto you, It is easier for a camel to go through the eye of a needle, than for a rich man to enter into the kingdom of God.*

met-a-phor n. A metaphor represents. It is a figure of speech in which a word or phrase that ordinarily designates one thing is used to designate another, thus making an implicit comparison, as in *"a sea of troubles,"* or *"All the world's a stage"* (Shakespeare). Also, connectors ("as" or "like") are not used. Isa. 40:6 ...All flesh *is* grass...; Ps. 23:1, *The* LORD *is* my shepherd; Matt. 26:26, *Take, eat;* this is my body. A metaphor resembles by using *"is"* instead of "like" or "as" which are used in similes.

me-ton-y-my n., pl. **me-ton-y-mies**. A figure of speech in which one word or phrase is substituted for another with which it is closely associated, as hyssop for blood in Ps. 51:7, *Purge me with* hyssop, *and I shall be clean.*

par·a·dox n. A seemingly contradictory statement that may nonetheless be true: *the paradox that standing is more tiring than walking.* 1 Tim. 5:6, *But she that <u>liveth</u> in pleasure <u>is</u> <u>dead</u> while she liveth.* Matt. 16:25, *For whosoever will <u>save</u> <u>his</u> <u>life</u> shall lose it: and whosoever will <u>lose his life</u> for my sake shall find it.*

per·son·ifi·cation n. A figure of speech in which inanimate objects or abstractions are endowed with human qualities or are represented as possessing human form; as in, "Hunger sat shivering on the road," or "Flowers danced about the lawn." Ps. 85:10, *Mercy and truth are met together; righteousness and <u>peace have kissed</u> each other.* James 1:15, *Then when <u>lust hath conceived</u>, it bringeth forth sin: and sin, when it is finished, bringeth forth death.*

sim·i·le n. A figure of speech in which two essentially unlike things are compared, often in a phrase introduced by *"like"* or *"as"* which are used as connectors, as in: *"How like the winter hath my absence been"* or *"So are you to my thoughts as food to life"* (Shakespeare). Isa. 53:6, *All <u>we like sheep</u> have gone astray...;* Acts 2:2-3, *And suddenly there came a sound from heaven <u>as of a rushing mighty wind</u>, and it filled all the house where they were sitting. 3) And there appeared unto them cloven <u>tongues like as of fire</u>...* A simile resembles.

Note: A parable can be formed by extending a metaphor or simile. It uses physical circumstances to present a spiritual truth. A figure of speech is simply a poetic way of expressing a literal truth.

sy·nec·do·che n. A figure of speech in which a part

is used for the whole (as "*hand*" for "*sailor*"), the whole for a part (as "*the law*" for "*police officer*"), Gen. 36:6, *And Esau took his wives, and his sons, and his daughters, and all <u>the persons of his house</u>.* Here the "*persons of his house*" are called the soul=*nephesh* which functions as a synecdoche. Gen. 42:38, *Then shall ye bring down my <u>gray hairs</u> with sorrow to the grave.* The gray hairs stand for <u>Jacob himself</u> in his old age.

The Berean Principle

Acts 17:11

"... they received the word with all <u>readiness</u> of mind, and searched the scriptures daily, whether those things were so."

© BWCT

ADAM AND EVE

And I will put enmity between thee and the woman, and between thy seed and her seed; it shall bruise thy head, and thou shalt bruise his heel (Genesis 3:15).

Welcome to the incredible story of God's love for those who love and hate Him. That's a strange introduction. Yes, it is. But God made this clear from the beginning. Creation consists of two different realms. What do I mean by that? Well, one is visible to us, and one is invisible. One is heavenly, and one is earthly. We have little perception of the first one because we can't see it, and God has not told us much about it. The heavenly realm is the place of angels, heavenly creatures, and Lucifer called the serpent and the devil. He became the enemy of God and those who love Him. In Genesis 3:15, God tells us of the two seeds. One would love Him, and the other would hate Him. It's a choice that creatures make, whether human or nonhuman.

When Adam and Eve put on the Sacrificial Garment provided by God, it pictured putting on the Lord Jesus

Christ in typology. Putting this in context with John 3:16 adds the background for God's great love story. Anyone saved by the grace of God experiences His love and has his own story to tell. The same was true with God's first created man and woman. So, to whom did Adam and Eve tell their salvation story?

Answering this question is simple, right? It's Cain and Abel. Let's imagine that we were their parents: How would we tell the story? Where would we begin based on what we know about God from His Word?

It might begin something like this — "Well, boys, God created the heavens and the earth in six days, and on the sixth day, He formed me from the dust of the earth and made me in His image and likeness. Then He breathed the breath of life into my nostrils, and I became a living soul. He placed me in a beautiful garden with trees with all manner of fruit. God gave me instructions and made me the caretaker. He permitted me to eat of all the trees but one. Then He warned me and said that I would die if I ate from it. Then God took one of my ribs, and from it, He made

Eve, your mother. Your mother is my helpmate, and together God told us to be fruitful and multiply and fill the earth with children like you and your sisters.

Just when things seemed to be at their best, everything changed."

"What happened," asked one of the boys? For the next few days, Adam and Eve explained what it meant to sin and how the knowledge of good and evil enslaved with shame and temptations. Then Adam and Eve explained how God, in His grace, came to them in the garden and offered them forgiveness by accepting His gift that foreshadowed Jesus Christ, the Lamb of God Who would die and bear the sins of all humanity. And one of the boys asked how they could receive the gift of forgiveness. Adam explained that sacrificing a lamb would be showing your faith in the blood of His future sacrifice for your sins. Abel spoke up and asked, "What is sin, Daddy?"

"Son, it is rebellion against God by not trusting and obeying Him. God made the first sacrifice for us, and we accepted it and put it on. We were willing to take off our fig leaves and place our faith in Him. Immediately God changed us inside, and His peace that we lost because of sin He renewed. That is what God taught us about the Sacrifice, and that's why we are teaching it to you. The day will come when God will ask you to bring a sacrifice."

Abel said, "Daddy, I can't wait," but Cain left with a look of anger. He would be the first of the God-haters. Adam and Eve came into the flesh by creation, and then every person afterward by a physical birth. Jesus makes it clear to all the need to be born of the Spirit (a second birth, born of God) in order to be a child of God and enter the kingdom of God (the eternal kingdom of righteousness in Rev. 21). Jesus taught Nicodemus that He is the Lamb slain from the foundation of the world. The entire conversation between Jesus and Nicodemus is given in John 3:1-21. He also taught him that He is the Son of God who would be lifted up as the Sacrifice first pictured in Gen. 3:21. In John chapter 3, Jesus revealed that He is that Sacrificial Lamb, the Scarlet Thread, in the Scriptures.

The elements of salvation present with the first souls saved are unchanging and consistent through the ages. No sinner will ever be saved without the blood of Christ and being born by the Spirit of God and then baptized (united together) into the body of Christ. One of many Scriptures teaching this truth is 1 Cor. 12:12-13, *For as the body is one, and hath many members, and all the members of that one body, being many, are one body: so also is Christ. 13 For by one Spirit are we all baptized into one body, whether we be Jews or Gentiles, whether we be bond or free; and have been all made to drink into one Spirit.*

Salvation is not dispensational. It is fixed by the elements given in Genesis 3:1-24. God's love, mercy, and grace are inseparable and are the first element. They are demonstrated in the second element, the Sacrifice, Christ. The third element is man's free will to respond to God's offer of salvation with repentance and faith (his faith). The substance of these statements is proven in Genesis chapters 3 and 4 with the responses of Adam, Eve, Cain, and Abel. Cain rejected the blood sacrifice.

The law, grace, and faith appear on the stage next in God's first act of salvation. The law is represented by the first commandment in Gen. 2:17, where God said not to eat of one specific tree. Sin and death came from eating that fruit. Grace came when Jesus offered them the garment of Sacrifice. Salvation came through repentance and faith when they took off the fig leaves and put on the Sacrificial garment by their faith.

The day is coming when Cain and Abel will offer their sacrifices. Might each of us understand and be able to identify the two seeds of Genesis 3:15 as we read the Scriptures? It is the key to understanding how people make their choices and what sacrifices they are willing to make to God. Jesus states what sacrifice we must be willing to give in this passage in Matthew 16:24-26, *Then said Jesus unto his disciples, If any man will come after me, let him <u>deny himself</u>, and <u>take up his cross</u>, and follow me. 25 For <u>whosoever will save his life shall lose</u> it: and <u>whosoever will lose his life for my sake</u> shall find it. 26 For what is a man profited, if he shall* *gain the whole world, and lose his own soul?*

The test of anyone's salvation experience is their willingness to surrender their will to God's will and follow His Son, even unto death if necessary. A person willing to do that is called a child of God, a follower of Jesus, and His disciple. All of the Lord's disciples were examples of this except one, Judas Iscariot, the serpent's seed.

Adam and Eve are the first examples of those who *put on the Lord Jesus Christ.* This pictured their salvation victory in Christ. The garments they put on required the death and sacrifice of another. God used this to teach them what they, in turn, taught their children.

Cain and Abel represent the two seeds of Gen. 3:15 as the story of salvation progresses through the ages.

Are you willing to lose your life for Christ? Can you honestly say that for me to live is Christ (He is my Lord), and to die is gain (because I will be with Him)? If so, pilgrim, your journey is truly blessed, and your future is as bright as His promise to be with you forever in His kingdom of righteousness in Rev. 21.

CAIN AND ABEL

And she [Eve] again bare his brother <u>Abel</u>. And Abel was a keeper of sheep, but <u>Cain</u> was a tiller of the ground (Genesis 4:2).

For folks like us who have a lifespan of only threescore and ten (70 years), and perhaps some with a bit more, a lot of time has taken place between chapters 3 and 4. The last verse in chapter 3 says that God drove Adam and Eve from Eden. Following in chapter 4:1-2, they have two sons with different occupations.

After Cain kills Abel and God judges him, we read this in Genesis 4:16-17, *And Cain went out from the <u>presence of the LORD</u>, and dwelt in the land of Nod, on the east of Eden. 17 And <u>Cain knew his wife</u>; and she conceived, and bare <u>Enoch</u>: and he builded a city, and called the name of the city, after the name of his son, Enoch.* The words underlined present points of interest to this author and most likely you also. Before we discuss these points, let's do some more thinking about the verse in our chapter title.

In the space between Genesis 3 and 4, God's presence remains with the first family.

Adam and Eve would have told their sons how God created them. They would have described the beauty of Eden. For sure, Adam would have spoken of his work as the garden's caretaker, and how God provided all the fruit trees that yielded an abundant food supply for their daily needs. Eve would have explained how she was the first mother of all humankind, and how God, their Creator, walked with them in the cool of the day in Eden. Then there would have been a sudden pause, a mournful sigh, and a trembling groan at the thought of the serpent's presence. The fall from innocence and the brokenness of their Creator's image must have been the most tearful page of their story.

The rest of the story is what shaped the different attitudes of both sons. Their views of God were totally different. Cain hated God. After all, God cast his father out of "Paradise Eden" and made him work by the sweat of his brow. These words must have run through his mind every day as he labored his God-cursed field: Genesis 3:17-19, *And unto Adam he said, Because thou hast hearkened unto the voice of thy wife, and hast eaten of the tree, of which I commanded thee, saying, Thou shalt not eat of it: cursed is the ground for thy sake; in sorrow shalt thou eat of it all the days of thy life; 18 Thorns also and thistles shall it bring forth to thee; and thou shalt eat the herb of the field; 19 In the sweat of thy face shalt thou eat bread, till thou return unto the ground; for out of it wast thou taken: for dust thou art, and unto dust shalt thou return.*

Cain must have been thinking something like this, "How could God do such a dreadful thing to my mother, father, and me, then when we get old, kill us?" A missionary who served in one of the Scandinavian countries of Europe told a very similar story as the one Cain may have perceived. He knocked on a door, and two middle-aged people asked him to come in. After a few words of introduction, he asked them if they had a Bible, and they said, "No!" So, the missionary gave them a Bible, and told them about Jesus and the gospel. The couple said they would like to read the Bible and invited him to come back in a few weeks. His follow-up visit was quite shocking. The moment he appeared at the door, this couple was furious and practically threw the Bible at him and said, "If your God kills two people for eating an apple, we want nothing to do with Him." And they slammed the door in his face.

This type of hatred and bitterness towards God is called *the way of Cain*, Jude 1:11, *Woe unto them* [the defiant]*! for they have gone in <u>the way of Cain</u>, and ran greedily after the error of Balaam for reward, and perished in the gainsaying of Core.* Cain killed Abel because he hated God. He is the first seed of the serpent. The serpent's seed is the wicked and ungodly, the devil's children.

Abel heard the same story as his brother. The story of salvation and God's love. He believed in the Sacrifice as told to him by his parents. Once a person is born of the Spirit, he experiences the love of God. Jesus appeared to people in a bodily form, as He willed. He spoke to Cain in his presence: Genesis 4:3-7, *And in process of time it came to pass, that Cain brought of the fruit of the ground an offering unto the LORD. 4 And Abel, he also brought of the firstlings of his flock and of the fat thereof. And the LORD had respect unto Abel and to his offering: 5 But unto Cain and to his offering he had not respect. And Cain was very wroth, and his countenance fell. 6 And the LORD said* [He was there talking to Cain] *unto Cain, <u>Why art thou wroth? and why is thy countenance fallen?</u> 7 <u>If thou doest well</u>* [bring the right Sacrifice], <u>*shalt thou not be accepted*</u> [you will be accepted]*? <u>and if thou doest not well, sin lieth at the door. And unto thee shall be his desire, and thou shalt rule over him</u>.* Only the Sacrifice of Christ and His blood will bring pardon and forgiveness of sin. Cain offered the work of his hands to God as a sacrifice, and it was rejected as said in Titus 3:5, *Not by works of righteousness which we have done, but according to his mercy he saved us, by the washing of regeneration* [born of the Spirit, the new birth], *and renewing of the Holy Ghost.*

Abel was willing, by faith, to live and die for his LORD. Shouldn't we all be willing to do the same?

CHILDBEARING

And Cain went out from the presence of the LORD, and dwelt in the land of Nod, on the east of Eden. And Cain <u>knew his wife</u> ... (Genesis 4:16-17).

Genesis 4 is perhaps one of the most intriguing chapters in God's Word. Why is this chapter so interesting? It is because of Eve's comments about the birth of Cain and because of Cain's wife. This verse in Genesis 4:1 gives Eve's remarks about her first son: *And Adam knew Eve his wife; and she conceived, and bare Cain, and said, <u>I have gotten a man from the LORD</u>.* Eve acknowledged that it was with the LORD'S help she had Cain. Many other women were praiseworthy for the LORD'S help as well. Probably Hannah is the most remembered with her prayer in 1 Samuel 1:11, *And she [Hannah] vowed a vow, and said, O LORD of hosts, if thou wilt indeed look on the affliction of thine handmaid, and remember me, and not forget thine handmaid, but wilt give unto thine handmaid a man child, then I will give him unto the LORD all the days* *of his life, and there shall no razor come upon his head.* The LORD answered her prayer, and Hannah said in 1 Samuel 1:27-28, *For this child I prayed; and the LORD hath given me my petition which I asked of him: 28 Therefore also I have lent him to the LORD; as long as he liveth he shall be lent to the LORD. And he worshipped the LORD there.* The LORD is good all the time, right?

The question about when Eve had her first daughter only has two possibilities. She either had daughters before Cain was born or afterward. For the former, there is no text. For the latter, there is. The fact that Eve is the mother of all living is proof that Cain married his sister. Here is the text for daughters in Genesis 5:4-5, *And the days of Adam after he had begotten Seth were eight hundred years: and he* [Adam] <u>*begat sons and daughters*</u>. *5 And all the days that Adam lived were nine hundred and thirty years: and he died.* So, Adam and Eve had three sons from sometime after creation to Seth (130 years), and afterward, they continued to have sons and daughters for 800 hundred years. 1

Corinthians 15:45 tells us that **Adam** was the **first man**: *And so it is written, The first man Adam was made a living soul; the last Adam* [Christ] *was made a quickening spirit.* Genesis 3:20 tells us that **Eve** is the **mother of all living**: *And Adam called his wife's name Eve; because she was the mother of all living.* That's where the human family begins.

What is interesting to note is the huge time gap before men and women had children. Here are a few examples:

Seth

Genesis 5:6-8, And <u>Seth lived an hundred and five years</u>, and begat Enos: 7 And Seth lived after he begat Enos eight hundred and seven years, and begat sons and daughters: 8 And all the days of Seth were nine hundred and twelve years: and he died.

Enos

Genesis 5:9-11, 9 And <u>Enos lived ninety years</u>, and begat Cainan: And Enos lived after he begat Cainan eight hundred and fifteen years, and begat sons and daughters: 11 And all the days of Enos were nine *hundred and five years: and he died.*

Cainan

Genesis 5:12, *And <u>Cainan lived seventy years,</u> and begat Mahalaleel: 13 And Cainan lived after he begat Mahalaleel eight hundred and forty years, and begat sons and daughters: 14 And all the days of Cainan were nine hundred and ten years: and he died.*

Noah

Genesis 5:32, *And <u>Noah was five hundred years old</u>: and Noah begat Shem, Ham, and Japheth. Genesis 9:28-29, And Noah lived after the flood three hundred and fifty years. 29 And all the days of Noah were nine hundred and fifty years: and he died.*

So what does it mean to be a child of God? It means to have a physical birth and then to be born of the Spirit by faith and surrendering your life to Jesus Christ, the LORD. That's how it started with all of Adam and Eve's children. How about you? Have you with a good and honest heart asked Jesus to deliver you from the wickedness of your sins, and are you willing to obey His Word and follow Him in a new life?

SETH AND THE SONS OF GOD

And to Seth, to him also there was born a son; and he called his name Enos: then began <u>men to call upon the name of the LORD</u> (Genesis 4:26).

Now is an excellent place to add some understanding about this word *LORD*. In many translations, LORD is used for the Hebrew name of God, which is *Yahweh*. This name comes from these words in Exodus 3:14, *And God said unto Moses, <u>I AM THAT I AM</u>* [He who is eternally self-existent]*: and he said, Thus shalt thou say unto the children of Israel, I AM hath sent me unto you.* God is known as the Great *I AM.* Moses was being commissioned to deliver the Israelites from Pharaoh, and he asked, "Who should I say sent me?" God's answer was *Yahweh*, the Great I AM. *Yahweh* is the <u>one name</u> used for all Persons of the Godhead — Father, Son, and Spirit. This verse puts that into context: Matthew 28:19 *Go ye therefore, and teach all nations, baptizing them in the <u>name</u> of the Father, and of the Son, and of the Holy Ghost.*

LORD, Lord, lord

"Lord," with the first letter capitalized in both Old and New Testament, is either the Hebrew word *Adonai* or the Greek word *Kyrios*. Jewish leaders started using *Adonai* for reverence and to avoid conflict with the Third Commandment: Exodus 20:7, *Thou shalt not take the name of the LORD thy God in <u>vain</u>; for the LORD will not hold him guiltless that taketh his name in <u>vain</u>.* The meaning of *vain* is to make common like Tom, Dick, or Harry. When "lord" was written in all lower-case letters, it referred to the master of the house or the person who employed someone.

In 1947, *Yahweh* was discovered in the *Dead Sea Scrolls*. Before that, Jehovah had been used as the Latin substitute since about A. D. 1278. It seldom appeared in most English translations until 1901. Charles Taze Russell, the founder of the Watchtower movement, was succeeded by Judge Rutherford. In the 1930s, he changed its name to Jehovah's Witnesses. Since that time, they have falsely promoted Jehovah as God's Sacred, Divine Name. Following is the definition of Jehovah in my 1983 dictionary: "Jehovah \ji-'hō-və\ *n* [NL, **false reading** (as *Yehowah*) of Heb *Yahweh*] (1530): GOD 1" *Webster's Ninth New Collegiate Dictionary* (9th ed.) (1983). Merriam-Webster Incorporated. As a substitute for God's personal name, Jehovah is in one sense the same as *Adonai*: It's a substitute.

When you read LORD in Scripture, it means *Yahweh*. When you read Lord, it refers to the one and only true God to whom you submit. When you read lord, it may refer to the person who employed you. If you are interested in learning more about the names of God and Who He is, you could find it in *The Trinity Book — What does it mean for God to be triune?* It is available at *Amazon.com*.

When people call upon the name of the Lord, they must know who He is. So, how did people in Adam's time learn about God? It began with the Lord Himself teaching them. We have already learned that the LORD, Jesus in a bodily form, was with Adam and Eve in the Garden of Eden, and He spoke to Cain before he slew Abel. The Lord did the same thing with Abraham and many others. Jesus gave the two men on the road to Emmaus these words in Luke 24:27, *And beginning at Moses* [Genesis 1:1] *and all the prophets, he expounded unto them in all the scriptures the things concerning himself.* Yes, it was Jesus that taught Adam and Eve the meaning behind the Sacrificial Garments they were wearing (a picture of Christ, as the Lamb of God dying for the sins of the world). He also taught them that salvation was through the Blood of the Sacrifice. Jesus' resurrection would fulfill the promise of Genesis 3:15. In each generation, God revealed more and more of His plan of salvation.

With the birth of Seth, the godly line or the seed of the woman was continued. These words were spoken by Eve at his birth in Genesis 4:25, *And Adam knew his wife again; and she bare a son, and called his name* <u>Seth</u>*: For God, said she* [Eve]*, hath appointed me* <u>*another seed instead of Abel*</u>*, whom Cain slew.* The godly line is recorded again by Luke. This genealogy traces Jesus' line back to Adam and God. Doing so connects the promises of Genesis 3:15, and the Abrahamic, and Davidic covenants to the entire human race. The genealogy starts with Joseph (the supposed father of Jesus) and ends with Adam in Luke 3:38, *Which was the son of Enos, which was the son of Seth, which was the son of Adam, which was the son of God.* When studying the two seeds, people are sometimes easily confused. It stems from two men named Lamech. One, the son of Methusael, a descendant of Cain, and the other, a descendant of Seth; the son of Methuselah, the father of Noah. Both sons were named Lamech.

In the history of Adam's children, there were seeds from both lines who chose to follow either the serpent or the woman's seed. Seth's first son Enos chose to follow his grandfather and father's faith in God's grace and His promise of salvation by the forgiveness of sin through His Sacrifice that He would provide for them. Scripture tells us that with Enos, people began to call upon the name of the LORD. The godly line was growing and continued until temptation gave way to the inward enemies of every person. You know what they are, right? You have heard them whispering to your soul words like this, "It's ok to look. It won't hurt to touch. Just try it you'll like it. No one knows but you; so what? You know better than they do." Yes, you know them; we fight every day: the lust of the flesh, the lust of the eye, and the pride of life. Then after you yield comes the guilt, shame, and sorrow. What makes the difference now is what one does next. Do you seek forgiveness from a merciful God Who loves you, or do you ignore the moment of decision and continue enjoying the pleasure and wickedness of sin? In Psalm 73, a son of God tells his story of how he was envious of the wicked. He came to his senses when going to the house of God and learning the fate of the wicked is eternal punishment and separation from God in the lake of fire. Then he realized his destiny with God was far better than anything this world could offer him. Sad to say that not all the sons of Seth and Enos felt the same way. What you are about to read is a continuous cycle. It finally ends in Revelation 21, where the saints find themselves on the new earth with Christ amidst the New Jerusalem on His throne, and there is no more sin, death, pain, sorrow, or crying. God makes all things new, and it will stay that way forever.

What you are about to read are some of the saddest words ever written:

Genesis 6:1-7

1 And it came to pass, when <u>men</u> began to multiply on the face of the earth, and daughters were born unto them,

Men in verse 1 are a reference to the seed of the serpent.

2 The <u>sons of God</u> saw the daughters of men that they were fair; and they took them wives of all which they chose.

Sons of God are the seed of the woman who defiled themselves with an unequal yoke. Sons of God cannot be angels because it would contradict Hebrews 1:5, *For unto which of the <u>angels</u> said He at any time, <u>Thou art my Son</u>, this day have I begotten thee? And again, <u>I will be to him</u>* [the angel] <u>*a Father, and he shall be to me a*</u>

<u>Son</u>? To be a son of God, one must be born of the Spirit, the second birth. Adam and Eve are the only exceptions: They were created.

3 And the LORD said, My spirit shall not always strive with man, for that he also is flesh: yet his days shall be an hundred and twenty years.

4 There were giants in the earth in those days; and also after that, when the <u>sons of God</u> came in unto the <u>daughters of men</u>, and they bare children to them, the same became mighty men which were of old, men of renown.

5 And GOD saw that the wickedness of man was great in the earth, and that every imagination of the thoughts of his heart was only evil continually.

6 And it repented the LORD that he had made man on the earth, and it grieved him at his heart.

There was no place in the hearts of these people for God. They had free will and chose evil rather than good. Romans says that God gave them over to a reprobate mind: Romans 1:28, *And even as they did not like to retain God in their knowledge, God gave them over to a reprobate mind, to do those things which are not convenient.* Proverbs remind us that as we think in our hearts, so are we. Then it also warns us to keep our heart with all diligence, for out of it can come both good and evil.

7 And the LORD said, I will destroy man whom I have created from the face of the earth; both man, and beast, and the creeping thing, and the fowls of the air; for it repenteth me [It grieved Him greatly to see us sinning] *that I have made them.*

In Genesis 6:7, the LORD has announced that He will cut off all those characterized as evil thinkers and doers. The people who perished in the flood had no fear of God until it came, and then it was too late. The Lord said it would be the same in the days just before His second coming in Matthew 24:38-39, *But as the days of Noe were, so shall also the coming of the Son of man be. 38 For as in the days that were before the flood they were eating and drinking, marrying and giving in marriage, until the day that Noe* [Noah] *entered into the ark, 39 And knew not until the flood came, and took them all away; so shall also the coming of the Son of man be.*

The truth in these words of Jesus ring throughout corridors of time and are seemingly fulfilled in every generation: Matthew 7:13-14, *Enter ye in at the strait gate: for wide is the gate, and broad is the way, that leadeth to destruction, and many there be which go in thereat: 14 Because strait is the gate, and narrow is the way, which leadeth unto life, <u>and few there be that find it</u>.* Our gracious Lord also promised this in Jeremiah 29:13, <u>*And ye shall seek me, and find me*</u>, *when ye shall search for me with all your heart.* The truth of this verse is never more than a prayer away. God would love to have more children. He is thinking of you. He has more love for you than you could ever imagine. His great love will enter your heart the moment you are saved and become His child. You will have a second birth and be born into the family of God by His Spirit. He will indwell you forever and be your Help and Strength in all your trials and hardships. He is greater than all your enemies from without and within. Yield all of yourself to Him, ask for forgiveness of your sins, and by faith, ask Him to save you now. And He will. What a Savior He is. Amen!

The Berean Principle

Acts 17:11
"... they received the word with all readiness of mind, and searched the scriptures daily, whether those things were so."

NOAH'S THREE WORLDS

Now all these things happened unto them for [examples]: and they are written for our admonition, upon whom the ends of the world are come (1 Corinthians 10:11).

The Lord has chosen some men and women to be His examples to encourage us all. Noah's heart was fixed in confident faith, and he was steadfast and unwavering in a lifetime lasting 950 years. He lived in three different worlds. When asked what it means to be a child of God, Noah's life answers that question with completeness. The LORD honored Noah's life and faithfulness by placing his name in the Hebrews 11 list of great men and women. Noah's long life gave him a testimony of loving obedience in times of unparalleled wickedness. God teaches us what one person can do in his lifetime who keeps his heart clean and has a desire to walk with God each day.

The Scripture says that all people know good and evil and choose one or the other. Those who love light more than darkness will seek the Lord and find Him:

John 3:19-21, *And this is the condemnation, that light* [the knowledge of good] *is come into the world, and men loved darkness* [the knowledge of evil] *rather than light, because their deeds were evil. 20 For every one that doeth evil hateth the light, neither cometh to the light, lest his deeds should be reproved. 21 But he that doeth truth cometh to the light, that his deeds may be made manifest, that they are wrought in God.* Noah was such a man.

Noah is perhaps the only person who lived in three worlds: before the flood, after the flood, and after Babel. Jesus spoke about him in Luke 17:26-27, *And as it was in the days of Noe* [Noah]*, so shall it be also in the days of the Son of man* [no fear of God or His judgment]. *27 They did eat, they drank, they married wives, they were given in marriage, until the day that Noe entered into the ark, and the flood came, and destroyed them all.* From my childhood until this day, I remember that people of this world do not talk about the flood. And by chance, if they do, it is a mocking denial of it. The world now is indeed like *the days of*

Noah.

The name Noah is Hebrew, and it means to rest or comfort. Names are what give people an identity. Scripture remembers Noah as a servant of God in many ways:

1. He lived in three worlds and walked with God in each of them.
2. He was a man of faith. He saw things no other man ever did.
3. He was blameless because his love for God was selfless.
4. He was obedient because doing God's will was foremost.
5. He was a husband. Scripture does not mention the name of Noah's wife.
6. He was a father. He had three sons, Japheth, Shem, and Ham.
7. He was the builder of the ark, which foreshadowed deliverance in Christ.
8. He was a preacher of righteousness, the salt of the earth, and a light in his worlds.

The LORD said that Noah was _perfect_ in Genesis 6:9, _These are the generations of Noah: Noah was a just man and perfect_ [blameless in a lifespan of 950 years] _in his generations, and Noah walked with God._

You might be thinking, "How does someone be perfect with God?" Enoch is the answer to that question. He walked with God: Genesis 5:24, _And Enoch walked with God: and he was not; for God took him._ A person who walks with God consistently keeps his heart right. He confesses sin and seeks forgiveness as soon as it happens. God is pleased to forgive him, and their fellowship is unbroken. That's what it means to walk with God or to walk in the Spirit. The LORD was so pleased with Enoch that he didn't die before leaving this world. He also pictures the rapture of the church before the seven years of great tribulation. The flood punished those mocking the coming of God's judgment. The Lord will do the same again in 1Thessalonians 4:13-17, _But I would not have you to be ignorant, brethren, concerning them which are asleep, that ye sorrow not, even as others which have no hope._

14 For if we believe that Jesus died and rose again, even so them also which sleep in Jesus will God bring with him. 15 For this we say unto you by the word of the Lord, that we which are alive and remain unto the coming of the Lord shall not prevent [precede] *them* [those who are already dead] *which are asleep. 16 For the Lord himself shall descend from heaven with a shout, with the voice of the archangel, and with the trump of God: and the dead in Christ shall rise first: 17 Then we which are alive and remain shall be caught up together with them in the clouds, to meet the Lord in the air: and so shall we ever be with the Lord.*

The LORD said that Noah was *just*. A just person is right with God. His heart is right because he has no unconfessed sin in his life. People who love God more than anything else keep themselves in the love of Christ, staying in right standing with Him. Job, Daniel, Hannah, Elizabeth, and Mary are other good examples. They were all people who hungered for righteousness, and God filled them. Every child of God could be like them.

The LORD said that Noah was *obedient*. Obedience is an act of love. Love is a choice. If love is not a choice, it has no binding power, and it is pointless. It has no real value to God or anyone else. Noah chose to obey God, and the Lord chose him to be an example. These verses in Matthew 22:37-38 characterize Noah's love for God; *Jesus said unto him, Thou shalt love the Lord thy God with all thy heart, and with all thy soul, and with all thy mind. 38 This is the first and great commandment.* These words describe Noah's love for God. The Lord is still looking for children like Noah in our generation. It can happen to anyone who has the want to. O Lord, give us many children and grandchildren now who have a heart like Noah's.

The LORD said that Noah was a *builder*. He was a builder in the most incredible sense concerning his character. His example is for all generations to follow. After living five hundred years, he had three sons, Japheth, Shem, and Ham. Before the flood, there was perfect harmony in Noah's family. After the flood, eight souls entered the new world, and everything changed.

Noah planted a vineyard, and he made wine and somehow became drunk. Most likely, it was not by his own doing, or God would have rebuked him. Noah, acting on God's behalf (now the dispensation of human government), cursed Ham and his son Canaan for their part in dishonoring him. Ham entered his father's tent and saw him (*uncovered and naked*). Ham went outside and told his two brothers. They took a blanket, put it across their shoulders, walked backward, and covered their father's naked body. When Noah awoke, he knew what had happened. But the LORD left the rest of the story untold.

There is a lot of speculation about the "how and what" in the verses below. The LORD chose the words He wanted to describe this awful day, and if we are wise, we'll add nothing to them. The comments may be missing from the text, but the results are marked by following Ham's bloodlines. God gave the land of Cannan to Israel, and His destruction of Sodom and Gomorrah represents the judgment pronounced on

Ham and Cannan.

These verses record the last events in Noah's life: Genesis 9:24-29, *And <u>Noah awoke</u> from his wine, <u>and knew what his younger son had done unto him</u>. 25 And he said, <u>Cursed be Canaan</u>; a servant of servants shall he be unto his brethren. 26 he said, Blessed be the LORD God of Shem; and Canaan shall be his servant. 27 God shall enlarge Japheth, and he shall dwell in the tents of Shem; and Canaan shall be his servant. 28 And Noah lived after the flood three hundred and fifty years. 29 And all the days of Noah were nine hundred and fifty years: and he died.* When we come to the life of Abraham, it will be important to remember who Canaan is.

The LORD said that Noah was a *preacher*. Noah was an excellent example like Abel. Before the flood, for a century, he warned the people of God's coming judgment of sin and was faithful for 350 years after the flood. We find these inspired words written by Peter in 2 Peter 2:5, *And* [God] *spared not the old world, but saved Noah the eighth person, <u>a preacher of</u>*

righteousness, bringing in the flood upon the world of the ungodly. God punishes the ungodly, not His children. Deliverance from the ungodly is why the rapture of the saints will occur before the seven years of great tribulation. Our assurance is in 1 Thessalonians 5:8-9, *But let us, who are of the day, be sober, putting on the breastplate of faith and love; and for an helmet, the hope of salvation. 9 For* <u>God hath not appointed us</u> [His children] <u>to wrath</u>, *but to obtain salvation by our Lord Jesus Christ.*

The LORD said that Noah was *a man of faith.* Noah is mentioned in the believer's hall of fame in Hebrews 11:7, *By faith Noah, being warned of God of things not seen as yet, moved with fear, prepared an ark to the saving of his house; by the which he condemned the world, and became heir of the righteousness which is by faith.*

Both Enoch and the family of Noah are God's examples to all of us. They pleased God and served Him with loving obedience. They escaped His wrath. He delivered them from the wicked. In this sense,

Noah's ark is pictured as a type of Christ. Enoch is pictured as a type of the rapture of the saints in Hebrews 11:5, *By faith Enoch was translated that he should not see death; and was not found, because God had translated him: for before his translation he had this testimony, that <u>he pleased God</u>.* The same could be true for every saint of God, right?

Scripture tells us that Noah lived in three different worlds. When the ark was unboarded, all its passengers set foot into the second world. The LORD had purged it from the curses of the previous one. It was a new beginning with a new covenant that God made with Noah. The LORD created a rainbow as a sign to mankind that He would never destroy the earth again by water. With Noah and his family, the LORD began a form of human government by creating the death penalty for murder. Instead of God dealing face to face with people, justice was to be carried out by men. Noah stands as one of the great, if not the greatest, of the Old Testament patriarchs.

As God-fearing people in the 21st century, we can

testify to the rise of wickedness that sets the great tribulation ever closer. Where are the people like Noah Whom God will, in their life span of *threescore years and ten*, say they were perfect (blameless) in their generation? People like Noah in our generation fit this description: They will work out their own salvation with fear and trembling. And the Lord will work in them both to will and to do of His good pleasure. They will do all things without murmurings and disputings. They will be blameless and harmless, the sons of God, without rebuke, in the midst of crooked and perverse nations, among whom they shine as lights in this world. They will hold forth the Word of life; that they may rejoice in the day of Christ. These words taken from Philippians describe the 950 years of Noah's life. He demonstrated his love for the Lord with all his heart, mind, and soul. Love is a choice, and he chose the Lord above all other things or people. Thank you, Noah! And it is my prayer that we will be found faithful like Noah. Amen!

THE GREATEST COMMANDMENT

Jesus said unto him, Thou shalt love the Lord thy God with all thy heart, and with all thy soul, and with all thy mind (Matthew 22:37).

Before we begin the next chapter, I would like to ask you two questions to think about with me. If loving God with all one's heart is the greatest commandment, wouldn't not loving Him with all your heart be the greatest sin? The second question is what I've been thinking the most about for a long time. Why would God have to make a commandment to tell people to love Him? When God's salvation story reached Genesis 22, I began to understand the answer to this question.

The first time I heard the love commandment was a few weeks after I was saved. A preacher on the radio quoted it, and immediately I was deeply grieved in my soul. I began speaking to the Lord by saying, "Lord, I know that I love my wife and children, I can't honestly say that I love You. I appreciate all that You have done for me, but to love You as commanded in this verse is something that You must teach me to do." That prayer was said nearly 50 years ago and is still my heart's desire.

From the first person, Adam, to Jesus and His disciples, personal contact with the Lord was key. Yet with some, personal contact did not always result in people loving Him more. Jonah is a prime example of why we must be told to love God. If you know the story, it won't be long before you figure out why. Just think about your own life as we all must do. The answer is in the verses after the greatest commandment. Matthew 22:39, *And the second is like unto it, Thou shalt love thy neighbour <u>as thyself</u>. 40 On these two commandments hang all the law and the prophets.*

One of the most important things to remember is that love is a choice. If it were not a choice, it would have no value. It would be worthless. When it is a choice, it is far above rubies. True love for others is priceless. God's love is pure and perfect because His love is selfless. The one and only eternal God is a God who exists in three persons, Father, Son, and Spirit. They love one another with perfect, selfless love. God created people to love and for people to love Him. He made man in His own image and likeness, and after the fall, that image was broken by sin. Sin is rebellion against God's Word and rejection of Him and His authority. Sin left man selfish and self-centered.

The love for self is why God had to command us to love Him. Loving our neighbors as ourselves is a constant reminder to put God and others before ourselves. The greatest hindrances to loving others are the lust of the flesh, the lust of the eye, and the pride of life. These enemies urge us to enjoy the pleasure of life without respect for the limits God has given us. When people love these pleasures more than God, eventually, they begin to hate Him. Why would they do that? Because there are consequences to sin, God will punish those who will not turn from it and do things His way, which is always best for everyone.

As the salvation story leads next to Abraham and Sarah, we learn from them that loving faith and obedience are what measure our selflessness and love for God as well as each other. As His Word and His Spirit sanctify children of God, our love for Him and others will steadily increase. It will be a great day for all of us when we can honestly say, as Paul did, "For to me to live is Christ and to die is gain."

The Lord recorded all these events in the Old Testament to help us. We can learn from these great men and women by their examples. It will help us grow spiritually and become more like Jesus each day of our lives if we do. Enjoy the next chapter, *THE BIRTH OF A NATION*. It is a nation that has eternal promises from God.

THE BIRTH OF A NATION

And thou shalt say unto Pharaoh, Thus saith the LORD, <u>Israel is my son</u>, even my firstborn (Exodus 4:22).

From the beginning of Genesis 4:1, the sons of Adam, Cain, Abel, and Seth chart the seeds of the woman and the seeds of the serpent: Genesis 3:15, *And I will put enmity between thee and the woman, and between thy seed and her seed; it shall bruise thy head, and thou shalt bruise his heel.* The enmity between the two seeds represents the battle between good and evil until the eternal kingdom of righteousness begins in Revelation 21. The woman's seed enters the new earth with their Savior, King Jesus, sitting on His throne in the New Jerusalem. The serpent's seed is cast into the lake of fire with the serpent himself, all the fallen angels, and every human being who chose darkness rather than light.

By the time of Genesis 6, just two chapters after Cain and Abel, the world had gotten so wicked that God purged it with the flood. Wickedness is what God saw in Genesis 6:5, *And GOD saw that the wickedness of man was great in the earth, and that every imagination of the thoughts of his heart was only evil continually.* After the flood, the earth was cleansed, and the soil was rich. Noah's three sons started producing children, but not all of them loved light more than darkness, and the serpent's seed began to multiply rapidly again. Ham violated his father, and his seed gave birth to a sin virus that once again contaminated the entire earth.

The birth of a nation is an entirely different chapter in the history of God's children. Why would I say that? It is different because Abraham's children's names are written above the gates of the New Jerusalem, the eternal city of God in Revelation 21. God's covenant with Abraham would be everlasting. Through Abraham, the woman's seed in Genesis 3:15 would crush the head of the serpent. His power of death as spoken of in Hebrews 2:14, *Forasmuch then as the children are partakers of flesh and blood, he* [Christ] *also himself likewise took part of the same; that through death he* [Jesus] *might destroy him that had the power of death, that is, the devil.* Genesis 3:15 was the mystery of the kingdom of God that had been concealed through the ages. Christ as the Seed of Abraham and David is what robed Adam and Eve in the Garden of Eden.

Would you take a moment and open your Bible and take the pages from Genesis 1:1 to Genesis 11:32 and hold them straight up towards the ceiling? What you see in these few pages is about 2000 years of history. Now do this again from Genesis 12:1 to Matthew 1:18, and you will have another 2000 years. Then go from Matthew 28:20 till the year 2022, and the periods are roughly about the same. Israel is still experiencing the covenant blessing God made with Abraham. Three great nations have come forth from Abraham's seed. From the descendants of Abraham's child bearers, Hagar, Sarah, and Keturah came Israel, Islam, and many unbelievers. From these three groups emerge children of God from all the nations and tribes of the world. Their stories give us the meaning of what it means to be a child of God by faith in Jesus Christ and the gospel containing His Scarlet Thread from Genesis to Revelation.

How all of this has come to pass, Jesus explained to His disciples in the parable of the sower. He described it as being the mystery of the kingdom of God, and for the most part, it is still a mystery today. Look at Mark 4:13-20, *And he said unto them, Know ye not this parable? and how then will ye know all parables? 14 The sower soweth the word. 15 And these are they by the way side, where the word is sown; but when they have heard, Satan cometh immediately, and taketh away the word that was sown in their hearts. 16 And these are they likewise which are sown on stony ground; who, when they have heard the word, immediately receive it with gladness; 17 And have no root in themselves, and so endure but for a time: afterward, when affliction or persecution ariseth for the word's sake, immediately they are offended. 18 And these are they which are sown among thorns; such as hear the word, 19 And the cares of this world, and the deceitfulness of riches, and the lusts of other things entering in, choke the word, and it becometh unfruitful. 20 And these are they which are sown on good ground; such as hear the word, and receive it, and bring forth fruit, some thirtyfold, some sixty, and some an hundred.* Jesus explained that three out of four people who heard the *word* were not born of the Spirit. He taught His disciples that being a Jew did not make you a child of God. He explained why in John 3:1-5, *Jesus answered, Verily, verily, I say unto thee, Except a man be <u>born</u> of water and of the Spirit, he cannot enter into the kingdom of God. 6 That which is born of the <u>flesh</u> is flesh; and that which is born of the Spirit is spirit. 7 Marvel not that I said unto thee, Ye must be born again* [born of God by His Spirit to be a child of God].

Abraham became a child of God the same as Adam did and as every other person must. The Scarlet Thread is the Blood of the Sacrifice, and Jesus Christ is that Sacrifice who gave His life's Blood to be the Savior of the world. Jesus, as the LORD in a bodily appearance, spoke to Abraham face to face as He did with Adam and Eve. Abram and Sarai were saved by faith in

God's spoken Word. We are saved by faith in God's written Word. In all cases, it is God's Word, as stated in Romans 10:17, *So then faith cometh by hearing, and hearing by the word of God.* So, as God delivers before our very eyes the birth of a nation that has eternal blessing, let us learn as Abram and Sarai did. As they grew in faith, God changed their names to Abraham and Sarah. Love is mentioned for the first time in the chapters of their lives. God allows us to see how He loves and teaches His children to love and worship Him through obedience. Enjoy the Birth of Israel.

The Berean Principle

Acts 17:11
"... they received the word with all <u>readiness</u> of mind, and searched the scriptures daily, whether those things were so."

© BWCE

NOAH'S GREAT-GRANDSON

And Cush begat Nimrod: he began to be a mighty one in the earth (Genesis 10:8).

The enmity between the children of God and the devil's children had its beginning with Cain and Abel. Now Noah's son Ham and his children start a new chapter in the saga of evil. It is important to remember that God's children have never won a battle against the seed of the serpent without the Lord's help.

Nimrod was the great-grandson of Noah. His father was Cush, the son of Noah's son Ham. Genesis 11 ends with the rise of the God-haters. Nimrod would raise a tower to reach the heavens. The tales of Nimrod are perhaps only exceeded by the tales of Mohammed. They both lived in the same area, had the same goals, and were mighty enemies of the woman's seed. Nimrod built a powerful kingdom that opposed God.

The connection between Genesis 11 and Genesis 12 continues until the end of Revelation 20. That connection stems from what Nimrod built. He was the devil's Job. Bible readers know the story of Job as being God's mighty servant. Well, Nimrod fulfills the same role as Satan's servant. It would not be unreasonable for the devil to have said to God, "Have you considered my faithful servant Nimrod?" What did Nimrod do? He built a powerful anti-God empire. He replaced Cain as one of the most rebellious God-haters who walked the earth.

The LORD brought Abraham from the devil's stronghold in Mesopotamia to Canaan, the place we call Israel. Genesis 15:7, *And he said unto him* [Abram], *I am the LORD that brought thee out of Ur of the Chaldees, to give thee this land to inherit it.* And Israel is still there today. Abraham triumphed for the same reason we can succeed: greater is He (the Holy Spirit) that is in us than the devil in this world. 1 John 4:4, *Ye are of God, little children, and have overcome them: because greater is He that is in you, than he that is in the world.* Thank You, Lord Jesus, for our victory over the serpent's seed.

ABRAHAM AT SEVENTY-FIVE

So Abram departed, as the LORD had spoken unto him; and Lot went with him: and Abram was seventy and five years old when he departed out of Haran. (Genesis 12:4).

Scripture tells us our trials of faith are more precious than gold. The life of Abram/Abraham brings this truth vividly before us. From these verses, we find the background of Abraham's family: Genesis 11:26-31, *And Terah lived seventy years, and begat Abram, Nahor, and Haran. 27 Now these are the generations of Terah: Terah begat Abram, Nahor, and Haran; and Haran begat Lot. 28 And Haran died before his father Terah in the land of his nativity, in Ur of the Chaldees. 29 And Abram and Nahor took them wives: the name of Abram's wife was Sarai; and the name of Nahor's wife, Milcah, the daughter of Haran, the father of Milcah, and the father of Iscah. 30 But <u>Sarai was barren</u>; she had no child. 31 And Terah took Abram his son, and Lot the son of Haran his son's son, and Sarai his daughter in law, his son Abram's wife; and they* *went forth with them from Ur of the Chaldees, to go into the land of Canaan; and they came unto Haran, and dwelt there.* Abram's wife was his half-sister: Genesis 20:12, *And yet indeed she* [Sarai] *is my sister; she is the daughter of my father, but not the daughter of my mother; and she became my wife.*

We learn more about Abraham (first known as Abram) and his family religion from this verse in Joshua 24:2, *And Joshua said unto all the people, Thus saith the LORD God of Israel, Your fathers dwelt on the other side of the flood in old time, even Terah, the father of Abraham, and the father of Nachor: <u>and they served other gods</u>.* This verse tells us about Abram's birthplace in Genesis 15:7, *And he said unto him* [Abram], <u>*I am the LORD that brought thee out of Ur of the Chaldees*</u>, *to give thee this land to inherit it.* The Chaldees were pagan worshippers of the moon god. Mohammed ruled this land in the seventh century and changed the moon god's name to Allah. There is much said about this in *The Islamic Invasion* by Robert Morey. It is incredible how little has changed in that area of the world since Abram left Ur of the Chaldees. At age 75, God speaks to Abram. The LORD was behind his father Terah's 600-miles move from Ur to Haran. Genesis chapter 11 closed with Terah dying when he was 205. Chapter 12 begins with the LORD speaking to Abram. He tells Abram to make another move from Haran to a land. What land? At this point, the LORD didn't say. But He did say this in Genesis 12:2-3, *And I will make of thee a great nation, and I will bless thee, and make thy name great; and thou shalt be a blessing: 3 And I will bless them that bless thee, and curse him that curseth thee: and in thee shall all families of the earth be blessed.* So, Abram obeyed, took Sarai, Lot, and all his belongings, and left Haran and, as we know, headed south.

Let's take a look at what the LORD promised to do for Abram if he obeyed Him:

1. I will make you (Abram) a great nation.
2. I will bless you richly.
3. I will make your name great.
4. I will make you the source of blessing to others.

5. I will do good to those who do good to you, and I will punish those who would harm you.

So, Abram departed as the LORD commanded him: *Get thee out of thy country, and from thy kindred, and from thy father's house, unto a land that I will show thee.* He may not know where he was going, but God said He would take care of him and bless him beyond his greatest expectations.

After Abram's big step of faith, this time, the LORD appeared to Abram and said this in Genesis 12:7-9, *And the LORD <u>appeared</u> unto Abram, and said, Unto thy seed will I give this land: and there builded he an altar unto the LORD, who <u>appeared</u> unto him. 8 And he removed from thence unto a mountain on the east of Bethel, and pitched his tent, having Bethel on the west, and Hai on the east: and there he builded an altar unto the LORD, and called upon the name of the LORD* [How did he call? With a surrendered life and obedient faith]. *9 And Abram journeyed, going on still toward the south.* He was headed for Canaan land, Jerusalem. This is Abram's second contact with the true and living

God, the Creator of all things. And He continues to increase Abram's faith through a personal visit. Don't you just love this? Intimacy is something God desires with all those who love and obey Him. Jesus explained this to Judas in John 14:22-23, *Judas saith unto him, not Iscariot, Lord, how is it that thou wilt manifest thyself unto us, and not unto the world? 23 Jesus answered and said unto him, If a man* [a person] *love me, he will keep my words: and my Father will love him, and <u>we will come unto him, and make our abode with him</u>.* That's exactly what the LORD is doing with Abram.

So, what happened when Abram called on the LORD in obedient faith and worshipped Him? Here's God's answer in Romans 10:13, *For whosoever shall call upon the name of the Lord* [like Abram did with a surrendered life and obedient faith] *shall be saved.*

In Genesis 22, this will change to loving, obedient faith. Love appears for the first time in Scripture when Abraham offers his only begotten son Isaac to the LORD, and this act personifies John 3:16 to the glory of God the Father and His only begotten Son, Jesus Christ.

Genesis 12 ends with Abram and his family going to Egypt because of a famine in Haran. He gets in trouble with Pharaoh because he refers to Sarai as his sister instead of his wife. Although she was his half-sister, she was also his wife. Because of Sarai's great beauty, Pharaoh decides to take her into his house. As a result, the LORD plagued him, and He was angry with Abram for concealing that Sarai was also his wife. Why did Abram do this? Was it his faith or lack of faith? Did the LORD rebuke Abram for his actions? No! Not this time or the second time when he did the same thing to Abimelech in Genesis 20. In both incidences, the LORD protects Abraham and Sarah and curses those who did them wrong. Both times the LORD sends Abram away with His blessings and great wealth as recorded in Genesis 12:20, *And Pharaoh commanded his men concerning him: and they sent him away, his wife, and all that he had.*

At ages 75 and 85, the LORD is just beginning to prove

to Abram and Sarai that there is nothing too hard for Him to do. These are faith-building chapters in their lives. It was not only the LORD'S Word that strengthened their faith, but it was also His presence that made the most significant impact. God was manifested in the flesh, and the disciples beheld His awesome glory. Each of them died a martyr's death (except for John) because of His presence in their lives. Now the Holy Spirit is that same presence in the life of those who are truly God's children. This truth is found in John 14:16; 26, *And I* [Jesus] *will pray the Father, and he shall give you another Comforter* [the Holy Spirit], *that he may abide with you for ever. 26 But the Comforter, which is the Holy Ghost, whom the Father will send in my name, he shall teach you all things, and bring all things to your remembrance, whatsoever I have said unto you.*

Abram and his family leave Egypt with more incredible wealth than one could have ever imagined. Abram, Lot, and Sarai have a lot to learn, and in each of the additional chapters, you can see it happening as their journey continues.

Genesis 13 marks the split between Abram and Lot. The LORD blessed them to the extent that the livestock flooded the land. Strife developed between the herdsmen, so Abram gave Lot his choice. He said that if you go left, I will go right, and if you go right, I will go left.

The choice Lot made is recorded here in Genesis 13:10-13. *Lot lifted up his eyes and beheld all the plain of Jordan that it was well watered every where, before the LORD destroyed Sodom and Gomorrah, even as the garden of the LORD, like the land of Egypt, as thou comest unto Zoar. 11 Then Lot chose him all the plain of Jordan. Lot journeyed east: and they separated themselves the one from the other. 12 Abram dwelled in the land of Canaan, and Lot dwelled in the cities of the plain, and <u>pitched his tent toward Sodom</u>. 13 But the <u>men of Sodom were wicked and sinners before the LORD exceedingly</u>.*

After Lot made his choice, the LORD took Abram and showed him the promised land, which is in part of modern-day Israel. Genesis 13:14, *And the LORD said unto Abram, after that Lot was separated from him, Lift up now thine eyes, and look from the place where thou art northward, and southward, and eastward, and westward: 15 For all the land which thou seest, to thee will I give it, and to* <u>*thy seed*</u> *for ever. 16 And I will make* <u>*thy seed*</u> *as the dust of the earth: so that if a man can number the dust of the earth, then shall* <u>*thy seed*</u> *also be numbered. 17 Arise, walk through the land in the length of it and in the breadth of it; for I will give it unto thee.*

Whose land is it? It's the LORD'S land. All the earth is the LORD'S, and He can give and take as He chooses as seen in Psalms 24:1-2, *The earth is the LORD'S, and the fulness thereof; the world, and they that dwell therein. 2 For he hath founded it upon the seas and established it upon the floods.*

Abram must have been blessed as the LORD continues to grow his faith. But as we know these words, *thy seed* will continue to trouble him until his laughter turns to joy some 25 years that are yet future.

Genesis 14 gives the account of Abram rescuing Lot and then his encounter with Melchizedek, King of Salem. In each of these chapters, we are looking to see how the LORD continues to build Abram and Sarai's faith. The LORD has blessed those who help Abraham and Sarah and cursed those who would harm them. God's protection assists Abram in anchoring his faith and triumph over his enemies, especially those attacking his nephew Lot.

The Eastern kings invaded the Jordan Valley and made war with the kings of Sodom and Gomorrah. Lot and his possessions were taken as part of their spoils. Then the survivors who escaped went to Abram for help. He puts together a force of about 300 of his own trained men and seeks to rescue Lot. He travels as far north as Dan, plans a night attack, and defeats them at Hobah. Abram recovers all the goods, including Lot, with his possession and all the women and other captives.

When Abram returns victorious, the king of Sodom goes out to meet him at the Kings Valley. And this is where Melchizedek, King of Salem, greets them. The significance of this meeting shows us how the LORD continues to increase Abram's faith. Not only his faith but his growing appreciation for the greatness of the LORD his God. God's promises to Abram are now becoming realities. He begins to testify of His greatness to the pagan king of Sodom. That is what follows in the dialogue of these verses in Genesis 14:18-24, *And Melchizedek king of Salem brought forth bread and wine: and he was the priest of the most high God. 19 And he blessed him, and said, Blessed be Abram* [a child of the King of KINGS] *of the most high God, possessor of heaven and earth: 20 And blessed be the most high God, which hath delivered thine enemies into thy hand. And he gave him tithes of all.*

After that, the evil king of Sodom wants to reward Abram for his victory. But remember what Scripture says about Sodom in the previous chapter: Genesis 13:13*, But the men of Sodom were wicked and sinners before the LORD exceedingly.* So Abram refuses his offer and states clearly why: *21, And the king of Sodom said unto Abram, Give me the persons, <u>and take the</u>*

goods to thyself. 22 And Abram said to the king of Sodom, I have lift up mine hand unto the LORD, the most high God, the possessor of heaven and earth, 23 That I will not take from a thread even to a shoelatchet, and that I will not take any thing that is thine, lest thou shouldest say, I have made Abram rich: 24 Save only that which the young men have eaten, and the portion of the men which went with me, Aner, Eshcol, and Mamre; let them take their portion.

Abram praises and glories in his God before this pagan king and says, "No deal!"

Chapter 15 opens with a new encounter with the LORD. The promise about Abram's seed continues to trouble him as the years go by, for Sarai is still barren. That seed will one day be Isaac. In the meantime, Abram is encouraged with these words in Genesis 15:1-3, *After these things the word of the LORD came unto Abram in a vision, saying, Fear not, Abram: I am thy shield, and thy exceeding great reward.* [The Lord is telling Abram that his reward for obedience will be very substantial.] *2 And Abram said, Lord GOD, what* *wilt thou give me, seeing I go childless, and the steward of my house is this Eliezer of Damascus? 3 And Abram said, Behold, to me thou hast given <u>no seed</u>: and, lo, one born in my house is mine heir.* The LORD told Abram that only one in his house would be the heir. At this time, Abram and Sarai do not have the faith to believe in the future Isaac. The LORD'S following words tell Abram that his heir will come from *his body*. His body may have led Sarai to her suggestion of young Hagar since Sarai was barren.

Then LORD took Abram outside and told him to look up into heaven at the stars. He asked him if he could count them and said that as the stars are in the sky, so will your descendants be. In the next verse, Abram says that he believes. Then the LORD God Almighty assures Abram with a covenant that his descendants will possess the land. At that time, God's impending judgment on the Amorites (Lot's descendants) will be satisfied. Joshua, after Moses dies, will lead Abraham's seed to victory in the promised land. This promise extends into our future with the Lord's victory at Armageddon. Abram asks the LORD how he could know for sure the land would belong to his heirs, and He doesn't hesitate to answer.

These are the answers the LORD gave to Abram in Genesis 15:6-18, *And he believed in the LORD; and he counted it to him for righteousness. 7 And he said unto him, I am the LORD that brought thee out of Ur of the Chaldees, to give thee this land to inherit it. 8 And he said, Lord GOD, whereby shall I know that I shall inherit it? 9 And he said unto him, Take me an heifer of three years old, and a she goat of three years old, and a ram of three years old, and a turtledove, and a young pigeon. 10 And he took unto him all these, and divided them in the midst, and laid each piece one against another: but the birds divided he not. 11 And when the fowls came down upon the carcases, Abram drove them away. 12 And when the sun was going down, a deep sleep fell upon Abram; and, lo, an horror of great darkness fell upon him.*

13 And he said unto Abram, Know of a surety that thy seed shall be a stranger in a land that is not theirs, and shall serve them; and they shall afflict them four hundred years; 14 And also that nation, whom they shall serve, will I judge: and afterward shall they come out with great substance. 15 And thou shalt go to thy fathers in peace; thou shalt be buried in a good old age. *16 But in the fourth generation they shall come hither again: for the iniquity of the Amorites is not yet full.* 17 And it came to pass, that, when the sun went down, and it was dark, behold a smoking furnace, and a burning lamp that passed between those pieces. 18 In the same day the LORD made a covenant with Abram, saying, Unto thy seed have I given this land, from the river of Egypt unto the great river, the river Euphrates.

Every promise the LORD has made is yes and amen! Enjoy your journey, pilgrims; we're headed for the promised land.

ABRAHAM AT EIGHTY-FIVE

And Sarai said unto Abram, My wrong be upon thee: I have given my maid into thy bosom; and when she saw that she had conceived, I was despised in her eyes: the LORD judge between me and thee (Genesis 16:5).

Chapter 15 ended with the LORD assuring Abram that the heir *shall come forth out of his own bowels*. Now, this is where Sarai begins to doubt that she will be the mother of that child. They had been in Canaan now for ten years. Abram is eighty-five, and she is seventy-five. Sarai's actions show that she genuinely cares about Abram's future and is willing to step aside as a barren woman and allow God's promise to happen some other way. Here is her suggestion to Abram in Genesis 16:1-3, *Now Sarai Abram's wife bare him no children: and she had an handmaid, an Egyptian, whose name was Hagar. 2 And Sarai said unto Abram, Behold now,* <u>the LORD hath restrained me from bearing</u>*: I pray thee, go in unto my maid; it may be that I may obtain children by her. And Abram hearkened to* *the voice of Sarai. 3 And Sarai Abram's wife took Hagar her maid the Egyptian, after Abram had dwelt ten years in the land of Canaan, and gave her to her husband Abram to be his wife.* Hagar seemed to be a good idea until she was expecting. Then Sarai became a reproach and was scorned. Sarai lost her self-dignity. It is important to note the time gaps in chapters 16 and 17. This is the first one in Genesis 16:3, *And Sarai Abram's wife took Hagar her maid the Egyptian, after Abram had <u>dwelt ten years</u>* [Abram is now 85; Sarai is 75] <u>*in the land of Canaan*</u>*, and gave her to her husband Abram to be his wife.* The second is in Genesis 16:16, *And Abram was <u>fourscore and six years</u> old,* [after Ishmael is born] *when Hagar bare Ishmael to Abram.*

The Sin of Presumption

Abram and Sarai's sin of presumption and its effect on others is the primary subject matter of this chapter. In chapter 15, the LORD assured Abram the heir would be of his *bowels*, but He did not mention Sarai in that dialogue. So Sarai thinks that Abram will lose his blessing because of her barrenness unless she does something. That is her presumption. The LORD clarifies this in chapter 18, and Sarah laughs.

Abram follows the same line of thinking and agrees to the alternate plan. That is Abram's sin of presumption. Abram could have taken God at His Word and told Sarai no. The lack of faith at any time leads to many bad decisions. Sarai now tells Abram, in so many words, "This is on you, and God will decide which one of us is at fault." Genesis 16:5, *And Sarai said unto Abram, <u>My wrong be upon thee</u>: I have given my maid into thy bosom; and when she saw that she had conceived, I was despised in her eyes: <u>the LORD judge between me and thee</u>.*

Abram doesn't hesitate a moment to tell Sarai, "Hey, this was your idea; you take care of the problem."

Next, the LORD intervenes and has compassion for Hagar. After all, she is just the handmaid in this family and has no say in matters like this. She is just a servant. The LORD tells Hagar to go back to Sarai and treat her with respect, and He will take care of the rest. Abram is 86 when Ishmael is born.

ABRAHAM AT NINETY-NINE

And when Abram was ninety years old and nine, the LORD appeared to Abram, and said unto him, I am the Almighty God; walk before me, and be thou perfect (Genesis 17:1).

In just a few lines of Scripture, thirteen years have passed. It must have seemed like an eternity for Abram. The LORD had not appeared or spoken to him since Ishmael was born. Abram had no Bible. There was no temple or synagogue to attend. Whether Abram prayed or had private devotions, the Scripture is silent. I don't know about you, but without the presence of the Lord, I would surely feel lost and forsaken. You might say, "But that could never be! How could anyone ever say what you just said?" Well, every child of God is born of the Spirit, and God speaks to His children in different ways at different times, but He speaks to all of them. The Holy Spirit was sent as our Comforter, Teacher, and Guide in the church age. A child of God will never be without His indwelling presence. Here's

how God's children know that is a reality:
1. Romans 8:16, *The Spirit itself* [Himself] <u>*beareth witness with our spirit*</u>, *that we are the children of God.*
2. Acts 8:29, *Then <u>the Spirit said unto Philip</u>, Go near, and join thyself to this chariot.*
3. John 14:16-17, *And I will pray the Father, and he shall give you another Comforter, that <u>he may abide with you for ever</u>; 17 Even the Spirit of truth; whom the world cannot receive, because it seeth him not, neither knoweth him: but ye know him; for <u>he dwelleth with you, and shall be in you</u>.*
4. 1 Corinthians 6:19, *What? know ye not that <u>your body is the temple of the Holy Ghost</u> which is in you, which ye have of God, and ye are not your own?*

Time for Thanksgiving

Thank You, Lord, for the Comforter, the Holy Spirit. Thank You for Your precious Word. Thank You for Your presence in us 24-7 and forever. Thank You for the Body of Christ and the fellowship among the children of God. Thank You for the freedom to assemble and worship together. Thank You for Your Church and the leaders You have called to guide it. Thank You for Your grace and mercy that allows us to experience Your love and presence in our lives each moment we live. Thank You for calling each of Your children to be Your witnesses in a lost and Godforsaken world. We love You, Lord, and will see You soon.

In Genesis 17 and 18, Abram and Sarai will have new names. Their laughter of doubt turns into the joy of Sarah's soon birth of a son in her old age of ninety years. The LORD will graciously increase Abraham and Sarah's faith in these chapters. The key to this kind of relationship is possible for those who will do as the LORD said in Genesis 17:1, *And when Abram was ninety years old and nine, the LORD appeared to Abram, and said unto him, I am the Almighty God;* _walk before me_ [in steps of obedience]*, and* _be thou perfect_ [is blameless, not sinless]. Walking before the LORD requires steps of loving obedience. Being perfect results from being blameless by having a clean heart with no unconfessed or unforsaken sin. From Enoch to Noah to Abraham and every person after them, the rule is the same. Who are the people who walk with God? All those who want to. Would you like to be one of them?

Names Changed

In chapter 17, the LORD changed names to reveal His will. Abram's name (exalted father) was changed to Abraham (father of multitudes). Along with the changing of his name came the sign of circumcision. It was the confirmation of His covenant with Abraham and all those of his household. Circumcision was explained in Genesis 17:5-14, *Neither shall thy name any more be called Abram, but thy name shall be Abraham; for a father of many nations have I made thee. 6 And I will make thee exceeding fruitful, and I will make nations of thee, and kings shall come out of thee. 7 And I will establish my covenant between me and thee and thy seed after thee in their generations for an everlasting covenant, to be a God unto thee, and to* thy seed after thee. 8 And I will give unto thee, and to thy seed after thee, the land wherein thou art a stranger, all the land of Canaan, for an everlasting possession; and I will be their God. 9 And God said unto Abraham, Thou shalt keep my covenant therefore, thou, and thy seed after thee in their generations. 10 This is my covenant, which ye shall keep, between me and you and thy seed after thee; Every man child among you shall be circumcised. 11 And ye shall circumcise the flesh of your foreskin; and it shall be a token of the covenant betwixt me and you. 12 And he that is eight days old shall be circumcised among you, every man child in your generations, he that is born in the house, or bought with money of any stranger, which is not of thy seed. 13 He that is born in thy house, and he that is bought with thy money, must needs be circumcised: and my covenant shall be in your flesh for an everlasting covenant. 14 And the uncircumcised man child whose flesh of his foreskin is not circumcised, that soul shall be cut off from his people; he hath broken my covenant.

Abraham Laughed

Why did Abraham laugh? Was it a laugh of faith or unbelief? The context answers this question for us. Let's take a look at Genesis 17:15-17, *And God said unto Abraham, As for Sarai thy wife, thou shalt not call her name Sarai, but Sarah shall her name be. 16 And I will bless her, and give thee a son also of her: yea, I will bless her, and she shall be a mother of nations; kings of people shall be of her. 17 Then <u>Abraham</u> fell upon his face, <u>laughed</u>, and <u>said in his heart, Shall a child be born unto him that is an hundred years old? and shall Sarah, that is ninety years old, bear</u>?*

The important thing here is not to misapply Romans 4:20, where it says that Abraham *staggered not at the promise of God through unbelief; but was strong in faith.* This verse is rightly applied only after Genesis 17:23 when the LORD reassured Abraham he would have a son by Sarah whose name would be Isaac which means laughter. God does have a sense of humor. After verse 23, Abraham *staggered not.* In Genesis 17:17, Abraham is staggering in unbelief.

Chapter 17 ends with a time stamp aging both Abraham and Ishmael in Genesis 17:24-25, *And <u>Abraham was ninety years old and nine</u>, when he was circumcised in the flesh of his foreskin. 25 And <u>Ishmael his son was thirteen years old</u>, when he was circumcised in the flesh of his foreskin.*

The Berean Principle

Acts 17:11
"... they received the word with all <u>readiness</u> of mind, and searched the scriptures daily, whether those things were so."

ABRAHAM AT ONE HUNDRED

Is any thing too hard for the LORD? At the time appointed I will return unto thee, according to the time of life, and Sarah shall have a son (Genesis 18:14).

Twenty-five years have passed since the LORD spoke to Abraham in chapter 12. And now, at one hundred years old, he has the joy of knowing that his God is the LORD God Almighty, Who can do anything. The timing of Isaac's birth magnifies Yahweh, Who is the LORD. Abraham and Sarah begin to see His infinite attributes described in Scripture. David speaks of God's omnipotence, omniscience, and omnipresence in Psalms 139:1-8, *O LORD, thou hast searched me, and known me. 2 Thou knowest my downsitting and mine uprising, thou understandest my thought afar off. 3 Thou compassest my path and my lying down, and art acquainted with all my ways. 4 For there is not a word in my tongue, but, lo, O LORD, thou knowest it altogether. 5 Thou hast beset me behind and before, and laid thine hand upon me. 6 Such knowledge is too wonderful for me; it is high, I cannot attain unto it. 7 Whither shall I go from thy spirit? or whither shall I flee from thy presence? 8 If I ascend up into heaven, thou art there: if I make my bed in hell, behold, thou art there.*

Sarah's Laugh of Unbelief

Remember how the LORD knew the thoughts of Abraham and Sarah's hearts though they had not spoken a word? Abraham laughed when God said Sarah would have his son when she was ninety. Sarah laughed at the same thought in Genesis 18:9-14, *And they said unto him, <u>Where is Sarah thy wife? And he said, Behold, in the tent</u>. 10 And he said, I will certainly return unto thee according to the time of life; and, lo, <u>Sarah thy wife shall have a son</u>. And Sarah heard it in the tent door, which was behind him. 11 Now Abraham and Sarah were old and well stricken in age; and it ceased to be with Sarah after the manner of women. 12 Therefore <u>Sarah laughed within herself</u>, saying, After I am waxed old shall I have pleasure, my lord being old* *also? 13* <u>*And the LORD said unto Abraham, Wherefore did Sarah laugh,*</u> *saying, Shall I of a surety bear a child, which am old? 14 Is any thing too hard for the LORD? At the time appointed I will return unto thee, according to the time of life, and* <u>*Sarah shall have a son*</u>*.* God knows every thought that people think. To some people, this isn't very comforting, but to others, it is. It is comforting because God has promised to give us the desires of our hearts when we delight in Him: Psalms 37:4, *Delight thyself also in the LORD; and he shall give thee the desires of thine heart.* Isaac gives this verse fulfillment to Abraham and Sarah.

Sarah's Denial

When the LORD said that Sarah laughed, she lied by denying it. I am sure she knew better the next time, for the LORD spoke this in reply: Genesis 18:15 *Then Sarah denied, saying, I laughed not; for she was afraid. And he* [the LORD] *said, Nay; but thou didst laugh.*

This part of Abraham and Sarah's life has a beautiful end and a new beginning. It's the beginning of a new chapter in the story of God's children. It adds greater substance to what it means for each of us to be a child of God. Thank You, Father, Son, and Spirit.

Genesis 21:1-8, *And the LORD visited Sarah as he had said, and the LORD did unto Sarah as he had spoken. 2 For Sarah conceived, and bare Abraham a son in his old age, at the set time of which God had spoken to him. 3 And Abraham called the name of his son that was born unto him, whom Sarah bare to him, <u>Isaac</u>. 4 And Abraham circumcised his son Isaac being eight days old, as God had commanded him. 5 And <u>Abraham was an hundred years old, when his son Isaac was born unto him</u>. 6 And Sarah said, God hath made me to laugh, so that all that hear will laugh with me. 7 And she said, Who would have said unto Abraham, that Sarah should have given children suck? for I have born him a son in his old age. 8 And the child grew, and was weaned: and Abraham made a great feast the same day that Isaac was weaned.*

Our God gives His children the privilege to call Him Father. He is longsuffering toward each of us. As a child, I remember a TV program called *Father Knows*

Best. Our Heavenly Father loves each of us with perfect love, and He knows what's best for everyone. He knew that Abraham and Sarah would both laugh because of the weakness of their faith. So, He named their son Isaac which means laughter. Isaac was a constant reminder to them to be strong in their faith because there is nothing too hard for the LORD.

One day, the LORD prompted my parents to call me David. And at age eight, our neighbor lady (who was a Christian) told me the story of King David, who defeated Goliath. As a child in an unsaved family, it was my first link to God. As a child of God, King David became endeared to me through reading the Psalms. One day we will meet and rejoice together about how our Heavenly Father brought us to His Dear Son, Jesus Christ, our LORD. Then I will be able to say as David did in Psalms 17:15, *As for me, I will behold thy face in righteousness: I shall be satisfied, when I awake, with thy likeness.* Amen!

ABRAHAM AT MOUNT MORIAH

Isaac said, My father, Behold the fire and the wood: but where is the lamb for a burnt offering? 8 And Abraham said, My son, God will provide <u>Himself</u> a lamb for a burnt offering (Genesis 22:7-8).

Many people could talk about God's story of salvation from Adam and Eve to the end of Revelation 20, and it would not equal the walk of faith taken by Abraham and Isaac to Mount Moriah. This place called Mount Moriah was later called Jerusalem, the city on a hill. It had the privilege of witnessing the story of salvation told in picture and Person. Abraham and Isaac would perhaps one day look over the banisters of heaven and see Jesus making His way to Mount Calvary and taking their place. To me, this is one of the most significant chapters in all of the Old Testament. As you read this chapter, you will feel something that only God's children can experience.

It's not a coincidence that love is mentioned here for the first time in Scripture. She cries out with all her passion and says to everyone that God so loved you that He gave His only Begotten Son so you might find salvation in Him. Because of Calvary, the world has a window to see the love of God. Someone may not understand what salvation is. It is the gift of God's offer with arms of love and grace. It is the invitation to leave your bondage of sin and guilt. Until now, you did whatever you wanted to do. The Lord wants you to trust Him and surrender your will and life to Him. He has a plan for your life. And He will walk with you as you yield your life to Him. Come and see how blessed it is to be a loving, obedient child of God.

The years have passed quickly since Isaac's birth. He is now a young man raised in a home filled with love and God's blessing. The day will come when God speaks to him in person. By now, Abraham has told him the many stories of how God became real to him and how he learned to trust and obey Him. This trip to Mount Moriah will never be forgotten.

The reason for their trip is given in the first verse of Genesis 22: *And it came to pass after these things, that*

God did tempt [test] *Abraham, and said unto him, Abraham: and he said, Behold, here I am.* God wanted to test Abraham's faith, trust, and love for Him. In the past, Abraham and Sarah both doubted whether God's promise of a son in their old age was possible. They both laughed at the possibility. Then the LORD asked Abraham this question: *Is anything too hard for the LORD?* When the child came, they were told to name him "Laughter." That's the meaning of the name Isaac. The LORD has a sense of humor even when correcting our unbelief. Abraham and Sarah's laughter turned into baby Isaac.

The question, "What does it mean to be a child of God?" is answered in part by one's faith. From Adam to Abraham, there was no Bible as far as we know. We also know that faith *cometh by hearing and hearing by the Word of God.* God spoke and appeared to people in their day as He willed. Christ sent the Comforter, the Holy Spirit, into the world to do the same thing for us: Acts 8:29, *Then the Spirit said unto Philip, Go near, and join thyself to this chariot.*

Faith and trust are the key elements that lead to love. What's the difference between faith and trust? Faith is taking God at His Word, and it's the bridge to trust. In Genesis 12, God told Abraham what He was going to do. In Genesis 18, He did it. Abraham and Sarah saw the LORD could do whatever was promised. Trust came by seeing God's promises that they believed were fulfilled. At the beginning of their walk of faith, it was simply a belief with no proof. God spoke to them, and they learned that He was trustworthy and able to keep His Word. At the end of Genesis 18, Sarah is 90, and Abraham is 100; they had Isaac. Trust is based on experience. Faith and trust make love binding in a marriage when someone says they love you. The result of faith, trust, and obedience are Abraham, Sarah, and Isaac's love for each other, and God, their Savior. What is about to happen on Mount Moriah is an example of John 3:16 speaking in the Old Testament. It personifies Calvary: *For God so loved the world, that he gave his only begotten Son, that whosoever believeth in him should not perish, but have everlasting life.*

Faith, Trust, and Obedience

Let's look at Genesis 22:1-19 verse by verse and see what it meant for Abraham to be a child of God:

1. *And it came to pass* [after many days] *after these things, that God did tempt* [test] *Abraham, and said unto him, Abraham: and he said, Behold, here I am.* God speaks directly to Abraham, and he answers. To those who walk with God, hearing His voice is one of the greatest blessings of being a child of God.

2. *And he said, Take now thy son,* <u>*thine only son Isaac*</u> [only son eligible to be the heir of God's promise to Abraham], *whom thou lovest, and get thee into the land of Moriah; and offer him there for a burnt offering upon one of the mountains which I will tell thee of.* Think of this command! Abraham is dependent on Isaac for the LORD'S promise to be fulfilled. If Isaac has no seed, the covenant is void.

3. *And Abraham rose up early in the morning, and saddled his ass, and took two of his young men*

with him, and Isaac his son, and clave the wood for the burnt offering, and rose up, and went unto the place of which God had told him. Without hesitation, Abraham obeys. He may be remembering his laughter of the past when he doubted. Then the LORD asked him this question: *Is anything too hard for the LORD?* What Abraham will do will be no surprise to the LORD. God's foreknowledge is what we often forget. Here is a good reminder: Revelation 13:8, *And all that dwell upon the earth shall worship him, whose names are not written in the book of life of the Lamb slain <u>from the foundation of the world</u>.* God knew from the beginning of creation who would receive and reject Him. God's salvation is a "whosoever will salvation." Trials are God's way of increasing His children's faith and blessing. What children like Abraham have is a desire to please their Heavenly Father. He wants to say the same thing about us as He did Abraham. We'll see this in a little bit.

4. *Then on the third day Abraham lifted up his eyes, and saw the place afar off.* His look was a look of faith. This time he knew his LORD could do anything.

5. *And Abraham said unto his young men, Abide ye here with the ass; and <u>I and the lad</u> will go yonder and worship, <u>and come again to you</u>.* The underlined words are Abraham's testimony of faith. His faith is telling him, "If I sacrifice Isaac, God will raise him from the dead."

6. *And Abraham <u>took the wood of the burnt offering</u>, and <u>laid it upon Isaac his son</u>* [his son's shoulders]; *and he* [Abraham] *took the fire in his hand, and a knife; and they went* [up the mountain] *both of them together.* Isaac is carrying the wood for the sacrifice. There are a lot of "ifs" here, but it is a clue to Isaac's age. His age could range from a young child, a young boy, to a young teenager. The latter is preferred by those who estimate Isaac's age. That being a

reference point, it would place Abraham at around 120 and Isaac around 20 years of age.

7. *And Isaac spake unto Abraham his father, and said, My father: and he said, Here am I, my son. And he said, Behold the fire and the wood: but <u>where is the lamb</u> for a burnt offering?* At this point, Isaac doesn't realize he is to be the sacrifice. If Isaac could have looked down the corridors of time, he would have seen Him. He is the Spotless Lamb of God, the only begotten Son of the Father, Jesus Christ. Adam and Eve's garments represent Him as the sacrifice for their sins. Isaac's willingness to lay down his life is a picture of what Jesus Christ did at Calvary for you and me and all sinners. Thank you, Lord!

8. *And Abraham said, My son, <u>God will provide himself a lamb</u> for a burnt offering: so they went both of them together.* What Abraham said about the Lamb is a timeless echo of God's love for every lost soul.

9. *And they came to the place which God had told*

him of; and Abraham built an altar there, and laid the wood in order, and bound Isaac his son, and laid him on the altar upon the wood. The Holy Spirit gave the writer of Hebrews these words as a commentary to what we read above: Hebrews 11:17-19, *By faith Abraham, when he was tried, offered up Isaac: and he that had received the promises offered up his only begotten son, 18 Of whom it was said, That in Isaac shall thy seed be called: 19 Accounting that God was able to raise him up, even from the dead; from whence also he received him in a figure* [as coming back from the dead].

10. *And Abraham stretched forth his hand, and took the knife to slay his son.* Isaac is a young man who trusts his father, Abraham. But there is much more to what you read here than meets the eye. We can only wonder how often Isaac's father and mother told him about the LORD their God. And that God promised him to be the heir to this great covenant. Isaac was obedient in

faith to his earthly father and his Heavenly Father, believing that he would be the covenant heir. Isaac heard God speak, which would be the beginning of a personal relationship with Him. Isn't our God wonderful?

The LORD calls on Abraham a second time in this chapter to assure him of the magnitude of his blessings: Genesis 22:15-19, *And the angel of the LORD called unto Abraham out of heaven the second time, 16 And said, By myself have I sworn, saith the LORD, for because thou hast done this thing, and hast not withheld thy son, thine only son: 17 That in blessing I will bless thee, and in multiplying I will multiply thy seed as the stars of the heaven, and as the sand which is upon the sea shore; and thy seed shall possess the gate of his enemies; 18 And in thy seed shall all the nations of the earth be blessed; because thou hast obeyed my voice. 19 So Abraham returned unto his young men, and they rose up and went together to Beersheba; and Abraham dwelt at Beersheba.*

ABRAHAM'S SERVANT

But thou shalt go unto my country, and to my kindred, and take a wife unto my son Isaac (Genesis 24:4).

In the previous chapter, Sarah was a hundred and twenty-seven years old, and she died. Abraham purchased the field of Ephron near Hebron for the price of four hundred shekels of silver and was deeded the property. Then Abraham, in his old age, makes plans to find a wife for Isaac.

Abraham and Eliezer

Abraham called for Eliezer of Damascus, his longtime faithful steward, and tasked him with finding Isaac a bride. What follows is a story with many spiritual lessons. Abraham remembered the promise of God's blessing to his seed. With that in mind, he plans to send Eliezer to his former country of Mesopotamia to find a spouse for Isaac from his father's family. Eliezer pledges with an oath to fulfill Abraham's wishes. But he said, "What should I do if the woman will not come with me?" Abraham answered him by saying: Genesis

24:6-8, *And Abraham said unto him, Beware thou that thou bring not my son thither again. 7 The LORD God of heaven, which took me from my father's house, and from the land of my kindred, and which spake unto me, and that sware unto me, saying, Unto thy seed will I give this land;* <u>*he shall send his angel before thee, and thou shalt take a wife unto my son from thence*</u>*. 8 And if the woman will not be willing to follow thee, then thou shalt be clear from this my oath: only bring not my son thither again.*

Faith and Prayer

Eliezer arrives just outside the city of Nahor (the home of Abraham's brother) and makes the camels rest by the well when the women draw water. And then he prays: Genesis 24:12-15, *And he said, O LORD God of my master Abraham, I pray thee, send me good speed this day, and show kindness unto my master Abraham. 13 Behold, I stand here by the well of water; and the daughters of the men of the city come out to draw water: 14 And let it come to pass, that the damsel to whom I shall say, Let down thy pitcher, I pray thee, that*

I may drink; and she shall say, Drink, and I will give thy camels drink also: let the same be she that thou hast appointed for thy servant Isaac; and thereby shall I know that thou hast showed kindness unto my master. 15 And it came to pass, before he had done speaking, that, behold, Rebekah came out, who was born to Bethuel, son of Milcah, the wife of Nahor, Abraham's brother, with her pitcher upon her shoulder.

The Prayer of Faith

Eliezer, what does it mean to you to be a child of God? The answer came immediately in the miracle of answered prayer when a beautiful, young, virgin, unmarried girl went down to the spring and filled her jar with water. Then Eliezer runs down to greet her and says: Genesis 24:16-20, *And the damsel was very fair to look upon, a virgin, neither had any man known her: and she went down to the well, and filled her pitcher, and came up. 17 And the servant ran to meet her, and said, Let me, I pray thee, drink a little water of thy pitcher. 18 And she said, Drink, my lord: and she hasted, and let down her pitcher upon her hand, and gave him drink. 19 And when she had done giving him drink, she said, I will draw water for thy camels also, until they have done drinking. 20 And she hasted, and emptied her pitcher into the trough, and ran again unto the well to draw water, and drew for all his camels.*

Wow! Don't we just love it when God answers prayer like this in our lives? Stop and think for a moment, then rehearse in your mind how many times the Lord did this for us. Perhaps you had the same reaction Eliezer did. He was dumbfounded and filled with amazement. He stood watching Rebekah wondering if she was the one for Isaac. She was, and Eliezer bows himself to the ground and worships the LORD. Rebekah returned with Abraham's servant, and it was love at first sight when Isaac saw her. They were married and began their lives together, walking with the LORD. Eliezer's mission was accomplished, and to God be the glory. Jesus taught the great lesson of this story when He said, *According to your faith be it unto you.* As we travel the same road of faith, what more do we need, pilgrims?

ISAAC, REBEKAH, AND JACOB

And he said unto him, What is thy name? And he said, Jacob. 28 And he said, Thy name shall be called no more Jacob, but Israel: for as a prince hast thou power with God and with men, and hast prevailed (Genesis 32:27-28).

Abraham died at the age of 175. Noah lived five lifetimes to Abraham's one. Noah died two years before Abraham was born. Each of them went to their graves with heirs who would continue bringing the Scarlet Thread closer to the starry skies of Bethlehem. These great heroes of the faith are the host of witnesses looking on to see who will take up the blood-stained banner and do their part to continue this incredible story of God's love and desire to walk and talk with His children. God still walks with His children who want to walk with Him. Did you know that includes you? Yes, you! Like Jacob, you need to have the <u>want to</u>. The want to is what made the difference between Jacob and Esau. It's what made the difference between John, who laid his head on the Lord's chest and heard the heartbeat of God. All these examples are here to inspire us to take advantage of God's desire to be personal and active in the lives of all His children. The Holy Spirit indwells God's children to make that possible. So, enjoy seeing it happen again with Jacob. There are four date stamps in these chapters. The one that's missing is Rebekah's. Date stamps usually arouse one's curiosity. Here they are:

1. Gen 24:7, Abraham dies at age 175.
2. Gen 24:20, Isaac marries at age 40.
3. Gen 24:26, Isaac was 60 when Rebekah conceived.
4. Gen 35:28, Isaac died at age 180.

The first struggle is Rebekah's barrenness. Some people may think that life is just a bowl of cherries when walking with the LORD. If you read Job's life story, you will have a different view of that notion. Walking with the LORD is an indication that you need Him. Learning to endure hardships is what makes one a good soldier. We need God's help. Proverbs 3:5-6 tell us how to get it: *Trust in the LORD with all thine heart; and lean not unto thine own understanding. <u>In all thy ways acknowledge him</u>, and he shall direct thy paths.* When these verses represent how one lives his life, that life will have God's blessing. Isaac showed his faith and trust by praying for Rebekah. The LORD honored his prayer, and she became fruitful.

One struggle led to another. Now the twins start struggling from birth: Genesis 25:22;26, *And the children struggled together within her; and she said, If it be so, why am I thus? And she went to enquire of the LORD. 26 And after that came his brother out, and <u>his hand took hold on Esau's heel</u>; and his name was called Jacob* [meaning heel or follow]: *and Isaac was threescore years old when she bare them.* Rebekah knew something unusual was happening, and she did the right thing. She took it to the LORD. That's a woman of faith.

Let's stop here before one makes the usual judgments about what Rebekah and Jacob do later. God, in His foreknowledge, knew how both of these boys would live out their lives. One had a passion for spiritual things, and the other didn't. So, who did God favor? The LORD gives Rebekah a "heads-up" in answer to her prayer. Rebekah got her response in Genesis 25:23, *And the LORD said unto her, Two nations are in thy womb, and two manner of people shall be separated from thy bowels; and the one people shall be stronger* [in a spiritual sense] *than the other people; and the elder shall serve the younger.* Now, for this prophecy to be fulfilled, Rebekah and Jacob became proactive. The commentators and many others take a dim view of their actions, but it is difficult to find their opinion expressed by the LORD. When Esau and Jacob's lives were over, didn't the LORD say He loved Jacob and hated Esau?

The following few Scripture verses reflect gap years, and we find twins at a significant turning point. Jacob begins struggling to be a man of God and the heir to Abraham's blessing. Only one of the twins will walk with God and become the heir to Abraham's blessing; Jacob was that person. Like his grandfather Abraham, he is willing to face the struggles and learn what it means to go from faith to trust to unquestionable obedience as a child of God. The chosen are the ones who take this path. Scripture says many are called, but few are chosen. Did you ever wonder why? Some people go from faith to salvation and stop there. That's enough! Faith responds to a promise. Trust comes when a promise is experienced like Isaac's. Unquestionable obedience came from offering Isaac. And God knows how far each person is willing to go. That is why the LORD becomes so personal to them in real life. The LORD came to Abraham, sat down, and ate the meal he prepared for Him. Jesus talked about this in John 14:22-23, *Judas saith unto him, not Iscariot, Lord, how is it that thou wilt manifest thyself unto us, and not unto the world? 23 Jesus answered and said unto him, If a man love me, he will keep my words: and my Father will love him, and we will come unto him, and make our abode with him.* Faith, trust, and loving obedience are what make the LORD'S presence a reality in the lives of His children. The same is true for you and me. Amen to that!

Birthright Then Blessing

Did you wonder what the difference is between birthright and blessing? The firstborn son typically held the birthright. That meant he was head of the household in the father's absence. He would receive a double part of his father's estate. On the other hand, the greater blessing is the covenant blessing as designated by God (Isaac vs. Ishmael, Jacob vs. Esau, Joseph vs. Ruben, and Ephraim vs. Manasseh, King David vs. Eliab, his oldest brother).

Jacob, like King David, was chosen by the LORD. He told Rebekah this in answer to her prayer. And He never rebuked Rebekah and Jacob for their passion in pursuing it. So, now that their plan is successful, the struggles begin because Esau threatens to kill Jacob. Rebekah insists that Jacob find a wife from her kinfolk. Then Isaac charges Jacob to take a wife from his mother's brother, Laban. Jacob stayed with Laban for 21 years and left with the LORD's blessing and many troubling memories of Laban's lies and deception. As he plans to leave, he gets word that Esau is seeking revenge.

While facing these perils, he cries out to God. Like his grandfather Abraham, Jacob will now see God face to face. And again, God becomes intimate and personal with those He has chosen. Here's the rest of the story in Genesis 32:22-30, *And he rose up that night, and took his two wives, and his two womenservants, and his eleven sons, and passed over the ford Jabbok. 23 And he took them, and sent them over the brook, and sent over that he had. 24 And Jacob was left alone; and there wrestled a man with him until the breaking of the day. 25 And when he saw that he prevailed not against him, he touched the hollow of his thigh; and the hollow of Jacob's thigh was out of joint, as he wrestled with him. 26 And he said, Let me go, for the day breaketh. And he said, I will not let thee go, except thou bless me. 27 And he said unto him, What is thy name? And he said, Jacob. 28 And he said, <u>Thy name shall be called no more Jacob, but **Israel**</u>: for as a prince hast thou power with God and with men, and hast prevailed. 29*

And Jacob asked him, saying, Tell me, I pray thee, thy name. And he said, Wherefore is it that thou dost ask after my name? And he blessed him there. 30 And Jacob called the name of the place Peniel: for <u>I have seen God face to face, and my life is preserved</u>.

Jacob to Israel

The LORD has said this many times: I am the God of Abraham, Isaac, and Jacob, and He now calls Jacob "Israel." It means having struggled with God, Jacob prevailed. It is a name that has characterized the nation of Israel to this very day. But as Jacob prevailed, Israel always will. She will rule again in the 1000-year reign with Christ, and her covenant blessings will pass into the eternal kingdom.

Part One — Salvation Stories will end here with this chapter. But the stories will continue until the end of Revelation 20. Those named in the Lamb's book of life will enter the New Earth and be with their Savior forever in His eternal kingdom of righteousness.

PART TWO — SALVATION DOCTRINES

The Berean Principle

Acts 17:11

"... they received the word with all <u>readiness</u> of mind, and searched the scriptures daily, whether those things were so."

INTRODUCTION

If any man will do his [the Father's] will, he shall know of the doctrine, whether it be of God, or whether I speak of myself (John 7:17).

If you were to go back and reread the chapter on The Authority of Scripture, it would relate to the thought Jesus mentioned in the above verse. What thought is that? It's the thought of knowing whether the doctrines are of God or men. This is what Jesus said about the Sanhedrin (the Jewish leaders of the people): Mark 7:7-8, *Howbeit in vain do they worship me, teaching for doctrines the commandments of men. 8 For laying aside the commandment of God, ye hold the tradition of men ....*

Jesus used the rules of context and harmony to refute the teachings of men. He used them when correcting the devil and Jewish leaders. When these rules are disregarded, the doctrines of men will replace the doctrines of God. Every generation experiences either the loss or gain of truth. What makes the difference are those who follow or ignore the rules. Without the rules, one can make any doctrine appear authentic. People who learn the rules and apply them will hear the Lord say, "Thou good and faithful servant, well done."

At the beginning of the church age, the Apostle John and the Apostle Paul were two of the most dedicated men in the battle for truth. The harmony rule is the law of no contradiction. It means truth that is God-given will never contradict itself. As we look at three different doctrines of salvation that divide Bible believers, you will see how the rules separate truth and error. The truth will always be found if truth means more to someone than anything else.

Here's a fresh look at some of the most simple rules everyone can understand, yet they are the most feared and rejected by those who teach doctrines of men.

1. Context Rule – The weaving together of words in phrases, sentences, paragraphs, chapters, or the entire Bible, which <u>can shed light on</u> and <u>adds to its meaning</u> in a passage, i.e., Rom. 3:10-18; Gen. 3:15; Psa. 14 and 53.

2. Harmony Rule – A truth that is God-given will always be in harmony with the whole of God's Word, i.e., Genesis. 3:21 *Unto Adam also and to his wife did the LORD God make coats of skins and clothed them.* 2 Pet. 2:1; 1 Joh. 2:2; 1 Tim. 2:1-4

3. Language Rule – The awareness of which language is being used in the verse, i.e., literal, figurative, or symbolic, and the grammatical functions that apply to each part of speech. John 8:58 Jesus said, *Before Abraham was, I am.* John 10:9 *I am the door...* Rev. 8:6 *And the seven angels which had the seven trumpets prepared themselves to sound.* A trumpet is the symbol of judgment. See "Ten Figures of Speech."

4. Grammar Rule – Recognizing and agreeing with gender and other grammatical rules that govern its interpretation, i.e., Eph. 2:8; 1Cor. 12:4-9

Three Doctrines of Salvation

1. Whosoever Will Salvation
2. Works Salvation
3. Sovereign Salvation

Genesis is the Bible's seedbed for doctrine. The

doctrine of salvation and its primary elements are given in Genesis chapters three and four. Salvation is the same for all those who become children of God. Every soul whose name is written in the Lamb's book of life will receive the gift of salvation as Adam and Eve did. God teaches the doctrine of salvation throughout the ages as He speaks to people one-on-one and through the prophets. Then, Jesus Christ, God manifested in the flesh, teaches His disciples to know the difference between the doctrines of God and men.

The doctrines of Christ and salvation are constantly under attack. And the rules of interpretation are the referees that guard the authority of Scripture. I just heard the official blow the whistle, and the action began. Please keep your eyes on harmony. He's headed downfield. Context blocks two contradictions, and doctrines of God score another victory over the doctrines of men. For a play-by-play review, just keep turning the pages.

WHY DO WE NEED SALVATION?

Wherefore, as by one man sin entered into the world, and death by sin; and so death passed upon all men, for that all have sinned (Romans 5:12).

Do you ever pause sometimes and think about what it must have been like for Adam and Eve to teach their boys about salvation? Put yourself in that situation. What would you have done? There are only four people on the planet. The question would be asked again and again throughout time, "What must I do to be a child of God (to be saved)?" The answer will always be the same. You must do what Adam and Eve did. What did they do? When the Lord came to them in the Garden, He went there with the law and grace. What does that mean? Well, the law demanded justice, and that was eternal death in hell, the punishment for Adam and Eve's sin. Grace said, because I love them, I will sacrifice Myself in their place. Adam and Eve said, "What do we do to receive Your grace?" And God said, *Now after that John was put in prison, Jesus* *came into Galilee, preaching the gospel of the kingdom of God, 15 And saying, The time is fulfilled, and the kingdom of God is at hand: <u>repent</u> ye, <u>and believe the gospel</u>* (Mark 1:14-15). The actual conversation that took place in the Garden is not recorded. But we do know the gospel in substance has never changed and never will.

In the beginning (Genesis), God appeared in a human form to Adam and Eve in the Garden. These appearances are called Theophanies and Christophanies. What do those words mean? They reference appearances of God (Jesus Christ) before His human physical birth in Bethlehem: John 1:14, *And the Word* [Jesus in John 1:1] *was made flesh, and dwelt among us, (and we beheld his glory, the glory as of the only begotten of the Father,) full of grace and truth.* What Jesus taught Adam and Eve about salvation is recorded in Genesis. The sacrifices of Cain and Abel are evidence that God made the way of salvation absolutely clear to them. Their salvation was in the Sacrifice of the animal that pictures Jesus Christ.

The difference between the two sacrifices is also a picture of the fig leaves. It was a bloodless means of covering guilt and sin. The garments that God provided required the shedding of the blood of the Sacrifice.

Born Of The Spirit

So, let's pretend for just a few minutes that you could zoom on your smartphone and ask Jesus this question, "Jesus, What must I do to be a child of God and be saved?" What could He possibly say? The most direct answer to that question is what He gave Nicodemus in John 3:1-7, *Jesus answered and said unto him, Verily, verily, I say unto thee, Except a man be <u>born again</u>, he <u>cannot see the kingdom of God</u>. 4 Nicodemus saith unto him, How can a man be born when he is old? can he enter the second time into his mother's womb, and be <u>born</u>* [physical birth]*? 5 Jesus answered, Verily, verily, I say unto thee, Except a man be <u>born</u> of <u>water</u>* [still physical birth] <u>*and*</u> *of the <u>Spirit</u>, he <u>cannot enter into the kingdom of God</u>. 6 That which is <u>born</u> of the <u>flesh is flesh</u>* [still physical birth]*; and that which is born of* *the Spirit is spirit. 7 Marvel not that I said unto thee, Ye must be born again.*

These verses make being born of the Spirit the only way one can enter into the kingdom of God. The kingdom of God begins in Revelation 21. This earth is destroyed, and new earth is created. All who will enter the kingdom of God have their names written in the Lamb's book of life. That list would include Adam, Eve, and all others who are born of the Spirit and are children of God. The Lord made this truth clear in some form to all generations. He made it most clear when He walked this earth and taught His disciples. The Lord made it especially clear in the gospel of John. Now the question of how does one become a child of God is answered first in John 1:10-13, *He was in the world, and the world was made by him, and the world knew him not. 11 He came unto his own, and his own received him not. 12 But as many as received him* [no limit], *to them gave he power to become the sons* [children] *of God, even to them that believe on his name: 13 Which were born, not of blood, nor of the will of the flesh, nor of the will of man, but of God* [by being born of the Spirit, John 3:6].

Faith

The verses above tell us to believe in His name (*Yahweh saves* or *Savior*) and receive Him. To believe in His name means to believe that Jesus is the eternal Son of God. It's to believe that He is the Savior, the Lamb of God Who died and was raised from the dead to pay for our sins and free us from their bondage. Jesus came to save people who wanted to be delivered from their sins. If that's not your desire, you don't need Jesus because you have not come to the point where you hate the evil that is part of your life.

Surrender

What does it mean to receive Jesus? It means to receive His Word and be willing to keep His Word. That means a change in who is in charge of your life. Before one receives Jesus Christ, you're the boss. You do as you will, whether it's God's will or not. That's called the law of your flesh. You obey it. To receive Jesus means you yield to Him. Your flesh loses its place, and

Jesus becomes the One you are willing to obey. Here's what Jesus said in two of the gospels: John 12:25-26, *He that loveth his life* [sinful life] *shall lose it; <u>and he that hateth his life in this world shall keep it unto life eternal</u>. 26 If any man serve me, <u>let him follow me</u>; and where I am, there shall also my servant be: if any man serve me, him will my Father honour.*

Jesus explains what it means to receive Him as Savior in Mark 8:35-37, *For whosoever will save his life shall lose it; but whosoever shall <u>lose his life</u>* [put your life in God's hands and surrender your will to Him] *for my sake and the gospel's, <u>the same shall save it</u>. 36 For what shall it profit a man, if he shall gain the whole world, and lose his own soul? 37 Or what shall a man give in exchange for his soul?*

The Wide Gate

To invite people to Jesus without asking them to surrender is the wide gate invitation to salvation or God's simple plan of salvation. The question is this: Are people willing to turn from their sins and follow Jesus? The simple plan changed the word repent to mean just confessing sins rather than having a desire to be delivered from them.

John the Baptist told sinners to confess their sins, turn from them, and seek God's righteousness. Admitting that you have sinned is not repentance. One must be willing to turn from sin. Confessing and turning from sin are two different gates. One is broad, leading to destruction. The other is narrow, leading to salvation.

The Lord said people could only serve one master, and He wants to be that Master. It won't work any other way. A person's most blessed life is one who has a desire to follow Jesus and obey His Word.

Jesus said in John 8:30-31, *As he spake these words, many believed on him. 31 Then said Jesus to those Jews who believed on him, If ye continue in my word* [with loving obedience and a hunger for righteousness], *then are ye my disciples indeed.* If you come to Jesus with an honest and good heart and are willing to follow His Words, He will save you. Do you want to be free from the bondage of sins? Is that what you want? Then come to Him now in prayer, and He will save you.

GENESIS SALVATION

If thou [God is speaking to Cain] doest well, shalt thou not be accepted? and if thou doest not well, <u>sin</u> lieth at the door. And unto thee shall be his desire, and thou shalt rule over him (Genesis 4:7).

Yes or No — It's Your Choice

Salvation in Genesis gives us all the elements associated with how a person is either saved or lost. It also shows the beginning of the enmity (hatred and warfare) between the two seeds of Genesis 3:15. There are two seeds or paths (good and evil) to follow, and each one makes choices. Since all people sin, good decisions can never restore and undo the bad. The people who choose a life of self-righteousness are the seed of the serpent. The people who accept Christ's righteousness on their behalf and yield their lives to Him are the seed of the woman. Cain and Abel show us all why some people are lost and some are saved. Cain offered the works of his labor, and Abel offered the works of Christ pictured in the Sacrifice of the

Lamb. The self-righteous people justify themselves by their own laws and deeds. What rules a person accepts is the difference between the doctrines (teachings) of men and the doctrines of God. Cain did what was right in his own eyes. Abel did what was right in God's eyes. His faith was in God's Word. Changing God's Word is what evil people do to make themselves right in their own eyes. The serpent was the source of Cain's deceived and bitter heart.

After the fall, Adam and Eve knew the voices of both good and evil. Then knowledge came to their hearts through the voices of the conscience. The evil voice is the serpent. He tempts our hearts to do bad things. The good voice is God, the Holy Spirit. He shows us the good things to do when tempted with bad. Remember the fig leaves to see the reality that fallen man always has a choice to do either good or evil. Adam and Eve put them on before the Lord spoke to them in the Garden. They were naked. Now, that was a bad thing because of the sin of lust and all the perverted varieties associated with it. Then came the shame. That was a good thing. It was the good Voice of the heart convicting of the right thing to do. Here are the two choices they had. They could have enjoyed the lust of their flesh and had a sex orgy, or they could do the good thing and covered their nakedness. Adam and Eve chose the voice of the Holy Spirit, convicting them to do right. Then they covered their nakedness with fig leaves. That covered their shame, but it did not remove the guilt and their fear of God's coming judgment of death. So, they hid from the Lord. Next, God came to them with His marvelous grace, and they made their choice and were born of the Spirit. All things became new, and the guilt and fear were gone. The Sacrifice was sufficient.

The first two people who received the Sacrifice and salvation were Adam and Eve. What was the sacrifice, and how did they receive it? It was garments made from animal skins. They received it by taking off their fig leave garments and putting on the garment God provided them. The animal garment required an animal's death by shedding its blood. That was a picture of what Jesus would do at Calvary. The garments God offered Adam and Eve represented the Sacrifice of Jesus Christ as the Lamb of God. So, Adam and Eve said yes to God's offer of salvation, and they were the first sinners born of the Spirit and became children of God. Then the Lord taught Adam and Eve about the Sacrifice and salvation, and they taught Cain and Abel.

Please remember in Genesis 3-4; it's just the beginning of Satan's work of deception. Cain and Abel are next on his list. He will continue to lie and cause people to doubt God's love and His Word. Adam and Eve's salvation gave them a new birth by the Holy Spirit, Who regenerated their soul and spirit and gave them new life. The guilt and shame were under the blood of Christ. They were forgiven, and they could tell their children salvation's story.

Cain And Abel

Cain and Abel are two children raised by the same mother and father. Their parents taught both of them salvation. The following verses reveal what happened next in Genesis 4:1-5, *And Adam knew Eve his wife; and she conceived, and bare Cain, and said, I have gotten a man from the LORD. 2 And she again bare his brother Abel. And <u>Abel was a keeper of sheep</u>, but <u>Cain was a tiller of the ground</u>.*

3 And in process of time it came to pass, that Cain brought of the fruit of the ground an offering unto the LORD. 4 And Abel, he also brought of the firstlings of his flock <u>and of the fat</u> [the animal was slain] *<u>thereof</u>* [it was a sacrifice]. *And the LORD had respect unto Abel and to his offering: 5 But unto Cain and to his offering he <u>had not respect</u>. And Cain was very wroth, and his countenance fell.*

Take a look at these comments about Abel's sacrifice in Hebrews 11:4, *<u>By faith</u> <u>Abel</u> offered unto God a more excellent <u>sacrifice</u> than Cain, by which he obtained witness that he <u>was righteous</u>, God testifying of his gifts: and by it he being dead yet speaketh.*

Why was Abel's sacrifice accepted, and why was it more excellent? It was by faith, representing his salvation in the Lamb of God, Jesus Christ. Why did

God reject Cain's sacrifice? God rejected Cain's sacrifice because salvation is only through the sinless blood of the Lamb of God. Like mom and dad's fig leaves, it was man's way of dealing with shame and guilt. <u>It was a type of works salvation.</u>

Cain got very angry; you might say he was boiling mad at God. The Lord asked Cain why he was so angry. And then the Lord told him that if he did right (brought the proper sacrifice), He would accept him. The Lord also said that if you ignore My Word about the Sacrifice, sin will overcome; you must master it. Cain then talks with Abel about what God had said, and when they were out in the field working, he killed him. See this dialogue in Genesis 4:7-8, *<u>If thou doest well, shalt thou not be accepted?</u> and if thou doest not well, sin lieth at the door. And unto thee shall be his desire, and thou shalt rule over him. 8 And Cain talked with Abel his brother: and it came to pass, when they were in the field, that Cain rose up against Abel his brother, and slew him.* Cain reveals himself as the seed of the serpent, and we know Abel was the seed of the woman according to Hebrews 11:4 and Genesis 3:15, *And I will put enmity between thee and the woman, and between thy seed* [the wicked] *and her seed* [the righteous]; *it shall bruise thy head, and thou shalt bruise his heel.*

Cain did have a choice, as Adam and Eve did, and as we all do. But he thought more of himself than he did of God. Jesus explained the nature of people like Cain. He said it was not that they were predestinated by God to be lost and didn't know or couldn't believe that kept them from being saved, but it was what they loved in their hearts in John 3:19, *And this is the condemnation, that light* [Cain had that light] *is come into the world, and* men loved darkness rather than light, *because their deeds were evil. 20 For every one that doeth evil hateth the* light [the seed of the woman], *neither cometh to the light, lest his deeds should be reproved. 21 But he that doeth truth cometh to the light, that his deeds may be made manifest, that they are wrought in God* [salvation through Jesus Christ].

Cain's sense of self-righteousness created his hatred for the Lord and those who followed Him. Just walk with Jesus through the gospels and especially read Matthew 23, and you'll see the same hatred for Jesus as Cain had for Him. Satan's enmity and those who follow him will continue until the end of Revelation 20.

The Berean Principle

Acts 17:11
"... they received the word with all readiness of mind, and searched the scriptures daily, whether those things were so."

LESSONS FROM GENESIS

And they which heard it, being convicted by their own conscience, went out one by one, beginning at the eldest, even unto the last: and Jesus was left alone, and the woman standing in the midst (John 8:9).

Knowledge of Good and Evil

We will reflect on what happened to Adam and Eve after they sinned. They are now lost: sinners. What made them different? Because of eating the forbidden fruit, God's commandment was broken, and the consequences were shame, fear, guilt, and death, both spiritual and physical. The knowledge of both good and evil brought conviction to their conscience. Good and evil are choices the conscience must deal with when faced with temptations. The wicked temptation would have been to ignore the shame and gratify the flesh with some perverse sexual activity. The good thing would be to cover the shame and hope for a way to deal with the guilt and fear later.

The lesson from Genesis is that fallen humanity does

have a moral compass, and as a sinner, he can do good instead of evil. It's a choice. But doing good cannot repair their broken image. What image is that? It's the image of God, their Creator, Who is righteous, sinless, and holy. Adam and Eve covered themselves with fig leaves to cover their shame. The conscience of sinners will convict them of good and evil. That's the way God made us. Before the Lord created us, He knew we would sin. The Holy Spirit speaks to our spirits and convicts us of sin, righteousness, and judgment as lost sinners. Our conscience is how He draws sinners to salvation. Genesis 1:26 tells us God made man in His image and likeness. God makes choices based on His will, and so do we. We were made in His image. The difference is that the Lord always makes the right choices, and we don't, as fallen creatures. But please don't forget we will be like Him again. In the resurrection, our choices will always be like His. Wow! I hear the glory bells ringing now.

So, as fallen sinners, Adam and Eve made a moral decision to do good. But without God's grace, they would be hopeless and lost forever. The guilt and fear of judgment would remain. That's why they hid from God. When Grace walked into the Garden and Love called out Adam's name, the Good Shepherd would find His first two lost sheep. Adam had no idea that day the meaning of Genesis 3:15, *And I will put enmity between thee and the woman, and between thy seed and her seed; it shall bruise thy head, and thou shalt bruise his heel.* When the Lord spoke these words to the serpent in Genesis 3:15, He also knew this in Revelation 20:10, *And the <u>devil</u> that deceived them <u>was cast into the lake of fire and brimstone</u>, where the beast and the false prophet are, and <u>shall be tormented day and night for ever and ever</u>.* Surely the devil did not know it then either, but he does now.

Genesis teaches us that temptation to do evil comes from the devil. He lied to Cain and made him hate God. How do you know that? Well, no one hates God without being told lies about Him. The devil tells people they can sin and get away with it. Look how he tempted King David to sin in 1 Chronicles 21:1, *And*

Satan stood up against Israel, and provoked David to number Israel. And David did so against God's commandment not to number Israel. Seventy thousand Israelites lost their lives because of God's judgment. The temptation to disobey God is a part of life. We know right from wrong, and when our spirit is tempted to do evil, Satan is the one behind it. He is at war with God and tries to use us as his allies. That's only possible if you surrender your will to him instead of the Lord. Just remember, "Greater is He (the Holy Spirit) that is in you than he (the devil) that is in the world." What we've learned about our spirit or conscience is one of the most important lessons in Genesis. It is how the Lord communicates with all sinners in their fallen state and shows them right and wrong. *The spirit* [conscience] *of man is the candle* [lamp] *of the LORD, searching all the inward parts of the belly* [being] *(Proverbs 20:27).* It is the Holy Spirit who indwells all God's children and empowers them to live victorious lives: Romans 8:16, *The Spirit itself beareth witness with our spirit, that we are the children of God.* His presence is Christ in us, the hope of glory. We, as God's children, have the opportunity to walk with Him each day and to dwell with Him forever. You may be thinking, "How do you do that?" The answer is: You just have to want to.

The Sacrifice

In the first few verses of Genesis 4, Cain and Abel are the subjects of the discourse. The text reveals their occupations. Cain works the soil and raises crops, and Abel is a herdsman and raises livestock. At some point, they both brought an offering (a sacrifice) and presented it <u>unto</u> the LORD. I will pause from the dialogue for a moment to mention something that is often missed. The phrase, *unto the LORD*, is often read without much thought, but here it is essential that <u>*unto the LORD*</u> be understood. The word "unto" indicates a motion towards a thing or person and then stopping at it. The LORD, in a bodily form, a Christophany, is still there with the <u>Adam and Eve's family</u>. You will lose much of the compassion the LORD shows towards Cain if you miss this. Reading Genesis 4:16 now will help establish the connection between the two passages: *And Cain <u>went out from the presence of the LORD</u>, and dwelt in the land of Nod, on the east of Eden.* Genesis 4:3, *And in process of time it came to pass, that <u>Cain brought</u> of the fruit of the ground <u>an offering</u> <u>unto</u> the LORD.* The LORD was standing in front of Cain as He did with Abraham and many others and reasoned with him.

In the verses you're about to read in Genesis 4, sacrifice is the keyword. The Sacrifice is what we believe in for our salvation. Jesus, Himself became the blood Sacrifice for all sinners, including those who rejected Him. Cain has rejected the Sacrifice picturing his salvation.

This verse in 2 Peter 2:1 makes it clear that the blood of Christ was shed for the false prophets and false teachers who rejected Him: 2 Peter 2:1, *But there were <u>false prophets</u> also among the people, even as there shall be <u>false teachers</u> among you, who privily shall bring in <u>damnable heresies</u>, even <u>denying the Lord</u> **that bought them**, and bring upon themselves swift*

180

destruction.

Cain's Sacrifice Rejected

Genesis 4:1-5

1 And Adam knew Eve his wife; and she conceived, and bare Cain, and said, I have gotten a man from the LORD.

2 And she again bare his brother Abel. And Abel was a keeper of sheep, but Cain was a tiller of the ground.

3 And in process of time it came to pass, that Cain brought of the fruit of the ground an offering unto the LORD.

4 And Abel, he also brought of the firstlings of his flock and of the fat thereof. And the LORD had respect unto Abel and to his offering:

5 <u>But unto Cain and to his offering he had not respect</u>. And <u>Cain was very wroth</u>, and his countenance fell.

The LORD Questions Cain

Genesis 4:6-7

6 And the LORD said unto Cain, <u>Why art thou wroth? and why is thy countenance fallen</u>?

7 <u>If thou doest well, shalt thou not be accepted</u>? and if *thou doest not well, sin lieth at the door. And unto thee shall be his desire, and thou shalt rule over him.*

Cain's reaction is similar to that of the prodigal son's brother. He was angry with his father because the father rejoiced over his sinful brother's return and repentance. The LORD was making it clear that if Cain brought the right Sacrifice, He would accept it.

Cain was a lost sinner who, by his own choice, knew that the LORD would accept him if he did right. So, was Cain a lost sinner because he could not choose to do right? The context rules that out completely. Was Cain forever a lost sinner because the LORD chose not to save him? The context rules that out as well. So, then, why do some people choose darkness (evil) rather than light (good)? Jesus answered that question clearly in John 3:19-21, *And this is the condemnation, that light is come into the world, <u>and men loved darkness rather than light</u>, because their deeds were evil. 20 For every one that <u>doeth evil hateth the light</u>, neither cometh to the light, <u>lest his deeds should be reproved</u>. 21 But he that doeth truth cometh to the light, that his* *deeds may be made manifest, that they are wrought in God.*

The LORD reproved Cain for the evil in his heart and gave him a choice to get it right. That's the same choice we all have. And we thank the Lord for His grace, love, longsuffering, and the truth that He is not willing that any should perish. 2 Peter 3:9, *The Lord is not slack concerning his promise, as some men count slackness; but is longsuffering to us-ward, not willing that any should perish, but that all should come to repentance.*

The Berean Principle

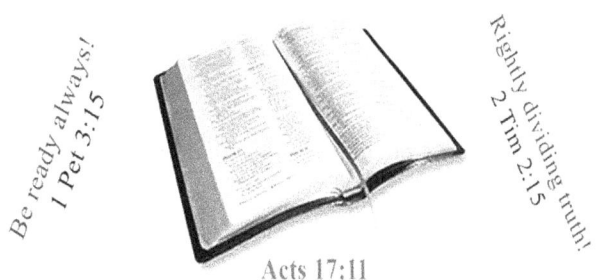

Acts 17:11
"... they received the word with all readiness of mind, and searched the scriptures daily, whether those things were so."

ROMANS 3 CONTEXT

As it is written, There is none righteous no, not one (Romans 3:10).

The clue to the context of Romans 3 is given in the first three words of verse 10: *As it is written.* Now is an excellent time to remember that Genesis 3:15 has an application to practically every chapter in Scripture, for it started in Genesis 3:1. The serpent lies to Eve to deceive her with the hopes of taking Adam's place as king of planet earth. His plan worked. He is called the god of this world. Let's put Genesis 3:15 in view to refresh our awareness of its permanent place in the history of humanity: *And I will put enmity between thee and the woman, and between <u>thy seed</u> and <u>her seed</u>; it shall bruise thy head, and thou shalt bruise his heel.* The serpent's seed is those who refuse to surrender to the LORD. The woman's seed is those who will surrender to the LORD and follow Him. The others follow the ways of the serpent. Here is one of the LORD'S many references to the two seeds: Matthew

13:38, *The field is the world; the good seed are the children of the kingdom; but the tares are the children of the wicked one.*

If you start reading Romans 1, especially verses 18-25, you will understand that Paul begins making it plain that no one can escape from the knowledge of both good and evil. Those without the law have conscience and creation. The Jews had the law and were trying to use it to justify themselves before God. Paul reveals to both lost Jews and lost non-Jews that there is no difference between them because they both have sinned and come short of the glory of God.

Let's look at, *As it is written* in Romans 3 first; then look at its context from Psalms 14 and 53.

Romans 3:10-18 Note: Only one seed is mentioned in these verses: the seed of the serpent.

10 As it is written, There is none righteous, no, not one:
11 There is none that understandeth, there is none that seeketh after God.
12 They are all gone out of the way, they are together become unprofitable; there is none that doeth good, no,

not one.

13 Their throat is an open sepulchre; with their tongues they have used deceit; the poison of asps is under their lips:

14 Whose mouth is full of cursing and bitterness:

15 Their feet are swift to shed blood:

16 Destruction and misery are in their ways:

17 And the way of peace have they not known:

18 There is no fear of God before their eyes.

Psalms 14:1-5 Note: Both seeds are mentioned in the context of these Psalms.

1 <u>*The fool*</u> *hath said in his heart, There is no God.* <u>*They*</u> [the fools] *are corrupt, they have done abominable works, there is* <u>*none*</u> [of the fools] *that doeth good.*

2 The LORD looked down from heaven upon <u>*the children of men*</u> [the fools]*, to see if there were any that did understand, and seek God.*

3 <u>*They*</u> [the fools] *are all gone aside,* <u>*they*</u> *are all together become filthy: there is none that doeth good,* [the fools] *no, not one.*

4 Have all the <u>*workers of iniquity*</u> [the fools] *no* knowledge? who eat up **my people** as they eat bread, and call not upon the LORD.

5 There were they [the fools] *in great fear: for God is in the generation of* **the righteous***.*

Seeds of the Serpent:

The fool, children of men, workers of iniquity, they (the workers of iniquity)

Seeds of the Woman:

My people (the children of God), the righteous

Psalms 53:1-5

1 *The fool hath said in his heart, There is no God. Corrupt are* they*, and have done abominable iniquity: there is none that doeth good.*

2 *God looked down from heaven upon* the children of men*, to see if there were any that did understand, that did seek God.*

3 *Every one of them is gone back: they are altogether become filthy; there is none that doeth good, no, not one.*

4 *Have* the workers of iniquity *no knowledge? who eat up* **my people** *as they eat bread:* they *have not called*

upon God.

5 There were <u>they</u> in great fear, where no fear was: for God hath scattered the bones of him that encampeth against thee: thou hast put <u>them</u> to shame, because God hath despised <u>them</u>.

Putting Romans 3 in context from the place where it was quoted makes it clear that the Genesis 3:15 enmity between the two seeds is the theme of Psalms 14 and 53. It says that fools like Cain have rejected God and continue persecuting His children. If one fails to put Romans 3 in its context, it could lead to a different opinion of mankind. Some might think that all people have rejected God instead of the fools who knew Him and killed His children. The fools were God-haters like Cain.

MANKIND'S MORAL COMPASS

Which [the gentiles] show the work of the law <u>written in their hearts</u>, their <u>conscience</u> also bearing witness, and their thoughts the mean while accusing or else excusing one another (Romans 2:15).

What we're about to discuss is a fascinating subject. God knew before He created us that we would fall. So, the way back from the fall was the knowledge of good and evil. Along with knowledge, He gave us a conscience. It works like a compass. It shows you what direction you are headed. The directions are good and evil. Something good will make you feel better. Something bad will make you feel terrible. Do you remember telling a lie and getting caught? How did you feel about that? Awful, right? How did you feel if you didn't get caught? Well, this is where a God-given conscience and the Holy Spirit convict you of sin, and you have a chance to make it right. What you do then will determine how you choose to live your life.

As a small child, I can remember telling a lie and

blaming my two-year-older brother. He was sent to bed after supper. When I went out to play that evening, I was all by myself, and I felt horrible. I never liked that feeling. It was guilt because I had sinned. It was then that I knew it was wrong to lie, for my <u>conscience convicted me it was a sin</u>. The same thing happened to Adam and Eve in the Garden when they sinned.

Once again, Genesis chapters 3 and 4 are the supporting context as Paul begins his dialogue on justification in Romans chapters 1-4. He is making the point about accountability for the unsaved Jews and Gentiles. He stated that there is no difference in their responsibility to God, for Jews and Gentiles that were lost knew God and had a choice to either reject or follow Him.

The Genesis accounts show that the first four people living on earth knew God after the fall and made moral choices to do good or evil. Adam and Eve put on fig leaves. They did that because they knew nakedness was evil. So, they did a good and moral thing and covered themselves.

Genesis 6 is where God draws the line for those who have rejected Him. Noah preached for a century, and then God said this in Genesis 6:3, *And the LORD said, My spirit shall not always strive with man, for that he also is flesh: yet his days shall be an hundred and twenty years.* They had sinned away their day of grace, and it was time for them to see the power of the Almighty God. The flood came and swept them away. These times of God's grace and longsuffering are repeated throughout the ages. Sodom and Gomorrah are other examples of the same fools that say, "No God." Paul is bringing this theme home in these verses in Romans in 1:18-21, *For the wrath of God is revealed from heaven against all ungodliness and unrighteousness of men, who hold the truth in unrighteousness; 19 Because that which may be known of God is manifest in them; for God hath showed it unto them. 20 For the invisible things of him from the creation of the world are clearly seen, being understood by the things that are made, even his eternal power and Godhead; so that they are without* *excuse: 21 Because that, when **they knew God**, they glorified him not as God, neither were thankful; but became vain in their imaginations, and their foolish heart was darkened.* They knew good and evil, and they chose evil.

These Scriptures declare that all people know that God exists by conscience or law and know good and evil. So, why do people reject God's grace and prefer to live in sin? Were they somehow programmed that way, or do they have a choice? Jesus answered this question clearly in John 3:19-21, *And this is the condemnation, that light is come into the world, and men loved darkness rather than light, because their deeds were evil. 20 For every one that doeth evil hateth the light, neither cometh to the light* [Why?], *lest his deeds should be reproved. 21 But he that doeth truth cometh to the light, that his deeds may be made manifest, that they are wrought in God.*

Love Is A Choice

Jesus said that choices are all about what one loves. Jesus explained this with the straight and narrow way that leads to life and the broad way that leads to destruction. Based on what you love, you will choose one or the other: Matthew 7:13-14, *Enter ye in at the strait gate: for wide is the gate, and broad is the way, that leadeth to destruction, and many there be which go in thereat: 14 Because strait is the gate, and narrow is the way, which leadeth unto life, and <u>few there be that find it</u>.* Who are the few that find it? Jesus answers that here in Matthew 10:39, *He that findeth his life shall lose it: and he that loseth his life for my sake shall find it* [everlasting life in Jesus Christ]. One loses his life by surrendering <u>his will</u> to do God's will. Now, you must see what Jesus said before verse 39. He said you would know how to be born of the Spirit of God and become His child: Matthew 10:37-38, *He that loveth father or mother more than me is not worthy of me: and he that loveth son or daughter more than me is not worthy of me. 38 And he that taketh not his cross, and followeth after me, is not worthy of me.*

God desires that all people would love and obey Him. But loving and obeying Him means we cannot love ourselves or others before Him. Our Creator and Savior deserves the throne of our hearts. He paid for us with His life-blood and suffered for our sins. He deserves our devotion. If love is not a choice, then it has no value. How would you feel if you were forced to marry someone you didn't love?

Jesus repeated this phrase to His disciples numerous times:

John 14:15, If ye love me, keep my commandments.

John 14:23, Jesus answered and said unto him, If a man love me, he will keep my words: and my Father will love him, and we will come unto him, and make our abode with him.

John 15:10 If ye keep my commandments, ye shall abide in my love; even as I have kept my Father's commandments, and abide in his love.

Matthew 22:36-38

36 Master, which is the great commandment in the law?

37 Jesus said unto him, Thou shalt love the Lord thy God with all thy heart, and with all thy soul, and with all thy mind.

38 This is the first and great commandment.

Your moral compass will direct you to the goodness of God, and it will lead you to surrender your life to a wonderful and loving Savior. Are you genuinely willing to trust His Word and put your life in His hands? If you are, please receive Him today by faith by taking off the fig leaves of self-righteousness and putting on Jesus Christ the Sacrifice for your sins.

What does it mean to be a child of God? It means to be born of His Spirit and on your journey to His eternal kingdom in a new heaven and earth that begin in Revelation 21:1-5, *And I saw a new heaven and a new earth: for the first heaven and the first earth were passed away; and there was no more sea. 2 And I John saw the holy city, new Jerusalem, coming down from God out of heaven, prepared as a bride adorned for her husband. 3 And I heard a great voice out of heaven saying, Behold, the tabernacle of God is with men, and he will dwell with them, and they shall be his people, and God himself shall be with them, and be their God.*

4 And God shall wipe away all tears from their eyes; and there shall be no more death, neither sorrow, nor crying, neither shall there be any more pain: for the former things are passed away. 5 And he that sat upon the throne said, Behold, I make all things new. And he said unto me, Write: for these words are true and faithful.

The Berean Principle

Acts 17:11
"... they received the word with all readiness of mind, and searched the scriptures daily, whether those things were so."

GRACE AND SALVATION

But God, who is rich in mercy, for his great love wherewith he loved us, 5 Even when we were dead in sins, hath quickened us together with Christ, (by grace ye are saved;)(Ephesians 2:4-5).

David asked the LORD these questions, "What is man, that thou art mindful of him? and the son of man, that thou visitest him?" He is mindful of us because we are the objects of His great love wherewith He loved us even when we were dead in sins. He gave Himself to take our place on the cross as unsaved sinners, meriting and deserving nothing. Christ suffered, bled, died, and rose again on the third day to conquer sin's penalty for *us*.

When the LORD walked to Adam and Eve in the Garden, He came with that great love in His heart. Out of that great love flowed the riches of His mercy and grace. When justice called for sin's payment, love sent mercy and grace to answer. Love, mercy, and grace come from the goodness of God and lead sinners to believe that Jesus <u>can</u> save them from shame, guilt, and sorrows of sins: Romans 2:4, *Or despisest thou the riches of his goodness and forbearance and longsuffering; <u>not knowing</u> that the <u>goodness of God leadeth thee</u>* [sinners] *to repentance* [with an honest and good heart to turn from sin <u>and a desire</u> to do right and keep God's Word]*?* Jesus described this in the parable of the sower in Luke 8:15, *But that on the good ground* [the fourth soil] *are they, which in an <u>honest and good heart</u>, <u>having heard the word, keep it</u>, and <u>bring forth fruit with patience</u>.*

Why would the good soil people want to keep God's Word? It's because by keeping the Word, they bring forth fruit and walk with the Lord each day. Is this how you would desire your life to be? If you are willing to follow Jesus, He will keep everything He promised to do for you. His love, mercy, and grace will follow you all the days of your life, and you will dwell with Him forever in His eternal kingdom of righteousness (Revelation 21).

FAITH THAT SURRENDERS

But they have not all obeyed the gospel. For Esaias saith, Lord, who hath believed our report? So then faith cometh by hearing, and hearing by the word of God (Romans 10:16-17).

To me, this is one of the most interesting subjects in Scripture. The verse above is the anchor in the sea of opinions regarding how saving faith comes to lost sinners. Some say faith comes by reading a nonbiblical book and experiencing burning in your bosom. Others say faith comes by speaking in an unknown tongue. Still, others say faith is imputed or delivered to those predestinated to be saved. And only these people will be saved. The rest will not be able to believe it. These are just three of the many versions of salvation in various religious groups. Thank the Lord for making the truth so clear and easy to understand in our chapter title verses.

When it comes to the subject of faith, nothing has changed much since Genesis 3:4-5, *And the serpent said unto the woman, Ye shall not surely die: 5 For God doth know that in the day ye eat thereof, then your eyes shall be opened, and ye shall be as gods, knowing good and evil.* That's what the serpent told Eve. He tempted Eve to doubt God's Word. Here's what God said in Genesis 2:17, *But of the tree of the knowledge of good and evil, thou shalt not eat of it: for in the day that thou eatest thereof thou shalt surely die.* The devil knows a lie is as good as the truth if you can get someone to believe it. Yep, there is great power in lies to persuade people to doubt God's Word. That's why God gave the rules to protect the authority of Scripture.

So, how did the deceiver break the rules that protect Scripture? He took a literal statement, *thou shalt surely die*, and made it figurative. What figure of speech did he use? It was an allegory. What is an allegory? It is a figure of speech using a picture, poem, or story that can be interpreted to have a hidden meaning. The trick is that only the person giving the allegory knows the hidden meaning. And that person was the serpent, and there was no hidden meaning, for it was a lie.

Our chapter title verses (Romans 10:16-17) rule out faith coming from the three different salvation versions mentioned above when put to the test. They are in harmony with the salvation stories beginning in Genesis and ending in Revelation. God spoke to them (some in person) and gave them His Word. So, their faith came by hearing and hearing by the Word of God. After that, for the most part, they read the Word, or the prophets spoke God's Word to them directly.

What Is Faith?

<u>Faith is believing</u>. Faith in God is your willingness to take Him at His Word and trust Him completely. His mighty works, goodness, and love for our souls are why we should trust His salvation. God sent His Son, Jesus, because He so loved people in this world.

We believe that the sun rises every day, in gravity, in time, and many other things that have proven reliable. We are willing to take people at their word and trust them unless they prove otherwise untrustworthy. Faith doesn't change; just objects of our faith are what change. If you are willing to fly in an airplane, drive a car, or wear a life jacket, it takes a measure of faith. What is believing? Believing is an action of the human heart resulting from our trust. God, above all others, had proven Himself trustworthy; therefore, He commands us to believe and trust Him. God cannot lie, and whatever He promises is guaranteed and will come to pass. All of this sounds so simple and uncomplicated. It is until the serpent tempts you to doubt or lies to you about the truth.

<u>What believing does</u> is explained in Hebrews 11:1, *Now faith is the substance* [the basis] *of things hoped for, the evidence* [proof positive] *of things not seen* [like heaven and the new earth]. Abraham believed in the New Earth, the New Jerusalem, and the Kingdom of God in Revelation, although he had never seen it. Still, he was looking for it as stated in Hebrews 11:10, *For he* [Abraham] *looked for a city which hath foundations, whose builder and maker is God.*

Faith And Salvation

The proof that salvation faith is an action of the human heart generated by our trust in God's Word comes from

Romans 10:8-11

8 But what saith it? The word is nigh thee, even in thy mouth, and <u>in thy heart</u>: that is, the <u>word of faith</u>, which we preach;

9 That if thou [you believing is the action of your heart, like anything else you believe] *shalt confess with thy mouth the Lord Jesus, <u>and shalt believe in thine heart</u> that God hath raised him from the dead, <u>thou shalt be saved</u>* [This is saving faith].

10 For with the [his heart] <u>*heart man believeth*</u> *unto righteousness; and with the* [his mouth] *mouth confession is made unto salvation.*

11 For the scripture saith, <u>Whosoever</u> [no limit like as many in John 1:12] *believeth on him shall not be ashamed.*

Who and how are lost people drawn to Christ? The answer to the "who" question is the Father, the Son, and the Holy Spirit.

John 12:32-33

32 And I, if I be lifted up from the earth, <u>will draw all men unto me</u> [no limit].

33 This he said, signifying what death he should die.

John 16:8

And when he [the Holy Spirit] is come, he will reprove the world of sin, and of righteousness, and of judgment.

John 6:44

No man can come to me, except the <u>Father</u> which hath sent me <u>draw him</u>: and I will raise him up at the last day.

The Centurion's Faith

Jesus used the faith of an unsaved soldier to shame Israel for their unbelief. The Centurion explained faith and why he believed Jesus could heal his servant in Matthew 8:5-10, *And when Jesus was entered into Capernaum, there came unto him a centurion, beseeching him, 6 And saying, Lord, my servant lieth at home sick of the palsy, grievously tormented. 7 And Jesus saith unto him, <u>I will come and heal him</u>. 8 The centurion answered and said, Lord, I am not worthy that thou shouldest come under my roof: but <u>speak the word only</u>, and my servant shall be healed. 9 For I am a man under authority, having soldiers under me: and*

I say to this man, Go, and he goeth; and to another, Come, and he cometh; and to my servant, Do this, and he doeth it. 10 When Jesus heard it, he marvelled, and said to them that followed, Verily I say unto you, <u>I have not found so great faith, no, not in Israel</u>. Believing Jesus is the Son of God and was the Creator of all things, what couldn't He do? The answer is: There isn't anything that God cannot do. The Centurion knew this when he sent for Jesus. So, once again, faith is simply taking God at His Word and trusting that He will save you when you surrender your will and life to Him.

Faith And Surrender

In Adam and Eve's salvation story, faith was the reason they put on the Sacrificial garments. Surrender was the reason they took off the fig leaves. They were willing to obey what the LORD was teaching them about salvation. Surrender is another word for repentance. Repentance is a change of mind and heart about sin and God. It's turning from self-will to God's will. Before I got saved, I was the boss. Afterward, I willingly submitted myself to God's will by finding it in His Word. The inward transformation was so wonderful that I never wanted it to stop and never will until I see Jesus. Then I will be like Him: 1 John 3:1-3, *Behold, what manner of love the Father hath bestowed upon us, that we should be called the sons of God: therefore the world knoweth us not, because it knew him not. 2 Beloved, now are we the sons of God, and it doth not yet appear what we shall be: but we know that, when he shall appear,* <u>*we shall be like him*</u>*; for we shall see him as he is. 3 And every man that hath this hope in him purifieth himself, even as he is pure.*

John the Baptist preached repentance, and when he passed on, Jesus began His ministry doing the same: Mark 1:14-15, *Now after that John was put in prison, Jesus came into Galilee, preaching the gospel of the kingdom of God, 15 And saying, The time is fulfilled, and the kingdom of God is at hand:* <u>*repent ye*</u> [you repent]*, and* [you] <u>*believe*</u> *the gospel.* God commanded all people everywhere to repent and believe in Him as Lord and Savior: Acts 17:30, *And the times of this* *ignorance God winked at; but now* commandeth all men [all people] *every where to repent.*

Jesus made surrender so simple with these words in Mark 8:34-38, *And when he had called the people unto him with his disciples also, he said unto them,* Whosoever will *come after me, let him* deny himself*, and* take up his cross*, and* follow me*. 35 For* whosoever will *save his* [not surrender] *life shall lose it; but whosoever shall* lose his *life* [surrender it to Me] for my sake and the gospel's*, the same* shall save it*. 36 For what shall it profit a man, if he shall gain the whole world, and lose his own soul? 37 Or what shall a man give in exchange for his soul? 38* Whosoever *therefore shall be ashamed of me and of my words in this adulterous and sinful generation; of him also shall the Son of man be ashamed, when he cometh in the glory of his Father with the holy angels.*

That is what God's Word has to say about faith and surrender. God will not save a person whose salvation doctrine differs from what you have just read. Is your faith like the Centurion's faith?

JESUS AND SALVATION

And ye will not come to me, that ye might have life (John 5:40).

The gospel of John begins with Jesus coming to His own people, the Jews, and them rejecting Him as the Messiah, the Son of God. Jesus told them to search the Scriptures if they thought they had eternal life, which testified of Him. Again, Genesis 3:15 and the two seeds could be the heading of just about every page in the Bible.

Why wouldn't people come to Jesus? Is the answer because they will not or could not come? If people choose not to come, the response agrees with *ye will not* and what Jesus said in the above verse. If people could not come, the answer disagrees with many verses in Scripture, including John 5:40.

As a start, the absence of choice would again conflict with the Genesis accounts and how God created man. What is meant by that? Well, let's take a look at Genesis 1:26-27, *And God said, Let us make man in our image, after our likeness: and let them have dominion over the fish of the sea, and over the fowl of the air, and over the cattle, and over all the earth, and over every creeping thing that creepeth upon the earth. 27 So God created man in his own image, in the image of God created he him; male and female created he them.*

The Will Of God And Man

One of man's likeness to God is his will. In the state of man's innocence, man's will was always in agreement with God's will. What's the difference between will and sovereignty? The will is the capability of conscious choice. Sovereignty, from God's standpoint, is absolute freedom from external control. God wills what He wills. From man's standpoint, sovereignty is he wills what he wills unless God intervenes. Perhaps the Jonah narrative is the best example of God and man's sovereignty. God tells Jonah to go to Ninevah and preach. The Jews and the Ninevites are arch enemies. Here is the conflict between God's will and Jonah's. Jonah boarded a ship headed in the opposite direction and jumped overboard to commit suicide. But God had a whale prepared to swallow him to teach him a lesson. God knew what Jonah would do before he did it. God also knew what all people would do before they were born. That is why nothing can surprise Him. His foreknowledge is the reason. He is an awesome and wonderful God. I am glad He knows all about me because He can help me with every problem.

Jonah had the sovereign will to make that decision but not the power to carry it out. The Jonah chronicle shows the difference between God's sovereignty and man's sovereignty. God allows mankind to do things He disagrees with within His permissive will, but all disobedience has consequences. God did not prevent Cain from rejecting His salvation and killing his brother. Did that plan of the serpent end the woman's seed? No, it didn't. Why? Because the sovereignty of man or the devil can never alter the sovereignty of God. How is that possible? It is possible because of God's foreknowledge. What is that? It is God's infinite (impossible to measure) knowledge of everything we think and do before it happens. Here is a verse revealing that in Revelation 13:8, *And all that dwell upon the earth shall worship him, whose names are <u>not written</u> in the <u>book of life</u>* [all the saved] *of the Lamb slain <u>from the foundation of the world</u>* [before the world existed].

When Jesus spoke of salvation, He invited all sinners to come to Him. He said that whosoever will or as many who will receive Him would become the children of God. Whosoever Will Salvation is what Jesus taught His disciples.

Whosoever Will Salvation

John 1:11-13

11 He came unto his own, and his own received him not.

12 But <u>as many</u> as received him, to them gave he power to become the sons of God, even to them that believe on his name:

13 Which were born, not of blood, nor of the will of the flesh, nor of the will of man, but of God [born of the

Spirit, John 3:3-7].

Luke 9:24

For whosoever will save his life shall lose it: but whosoever will lose his life for my sake, the same shall save it.

1 Timothy 2:3-4

3 For this is good and acceptable in the sight of God our Savior [Jesus Christ];

4 [Jesus] *Who will have all men to be saved, and to come unto the knowledge of the truth.*

2 Peter 3:9

The Lord is not slack concerning his promise, as some men count slackness; but is longsuffering to us-ward, not willing that any should perish, but that all should come to repentance.

Revelation 22:16-17

16 I Jesus have sent mine angel to testify unto you these things in the churches. I am the root and the offspring of David, and the bright and morning star.

17 And the Spirit and the bride [the saved] *say, Come. And let him that heareth say, Come. And let him that is* _athirst come. And whosoever will, let him take the water of life freely._

God extended salvation to all people. He proved Himself trustworthy by His holiness, love, goodness, and mighty works; therefore, He calls on us to come to Him in faith with a willingness to follow Him and His Word. It is surrendering your life and will with an honest and good heart to keep His Word and become fruitful for His honor and glory: Luke 8:15, *But that on the good ground are they, which in an honest and good heart, having heard the word, keep it, and bring forth fruit with patience.* The Holy Spirit and your obedience to God's Word will transform you into a new creature: 2 Corinthians 5:17, *Therefore if any man* [person] *be in Christ, he* [that person] *is a new creature: old things are passed away; behold, all things are become new.* That's the miracle of a new birth and becoming a child of God and a child of His kingdom (Revelation 21).

Sovereign Salvation

What is the difference between Whosoever Will

Salvation and Sovereign Salvation? Whosoever Will Salvation began in Genesis with Adam and Eve. Jesus and the Apostles taught it. It is in harmony with the rules which guard the authority of Scripture. Sovereign salvation is not. It's a teaching of man that can be traced to Tertullian (155 AD – 220 AD), The Church of Rome and Augustine of Hippo (354 AD – 430 AD), Martin Luther, an Augustinian Monk (1483 AD – 1546 AD), John Calvin, mentored by Luther, Charles Spurgeon (1834 AD – 1892 AD)[1], and many others. Sovereign Salvation comes from the notion of total depravity and predestination. Without the teaching of total depravity, sovereign salvation would not exist. Total depravity is the idea that Adam, Eve, and all mankind, after they sinned, no longer knew both good and evil (they only knew evil), making it impossible for them to have a desire to be delivered from their sins. So, "God predestinating sinners" is their only means of salvation.

---

[1] en.m.wikipedia.org/

So, why is Sovereign Salvation wrong? It is incorrect for the following reasons:

1. It restricts or alters God's attribute of omniscience (the state of knowing everything before it happens). Before the earth and world were ever created, God knew who would be willing to surrender their lives to His Son and who wouldn't: Revelation 13:8, *And all that dwell upon the earth shall worship him, whose names are not written in the book of life of the Lamb slain from the foundation of the world.* God chose the *elect* to be His children because of His foreknowledge: 1 Peter 1:2, *Elect according to the foreknowledge of God the Father, through sanctification of the Spirit, unto obedience and sprinkling of the blood of Jesus Christ: Grace unto you, and peace, be multiplied.*
2. It changes the extent of God's love and denies it to those not predestined to salvation. It contradicts the most well-known verse in the

Bible: John 3:16, *For God so loved the world, that he gave his only begotten Son, that whosoever* [grace to all] *believeth in him should not perish, but have everlasting life.*

3. It limits Christ's blood atonement to the predestinated. It contradicts the truth in both of these verses: 2 Peter 2:1, *But there were false prophets also among the people, even as there shall be false teachers among you, who privily shall bring in damnable heresies, even denying the Lord that bought them, and bring upon themselves swift destruction.* 1 John 2:2, *And he is the propitiation for our sins: and not for ours only, but also for the sins of the whole world.*

When it comes to the doctrine of salvation, none of the men mentioned in the first paragraph applied the God-given rules that would have protected them from altering the truth of God's character and His Word.

Elect According To Foreknowledge

Elect appears 17 times in the Bible, and it means to choose. The first place is in Isaiah 42:1, and it is a reference to Jesus Christ, the Messiah, God's Son: *Behold my* [God the Father speaking] *servant, whom I uphold; mine elect* [the Messiah, Christ], *in whom my soul delighteth; I have put my spirit upon him: he shall bring forth judgment to the Gentiles.* God's elect is the ones He chooses. The most important truth to acknowledge is how God elects His chosen. 1 Peter 1:1-2 tells how God elects: *Peter, an apostle of Jesus Christ, to the strangers* [Christians] *scattered throughout Pontus, Galatia, Cappadocia, Asia, and Bithynia, 2* <u>*Elect according to the foreknowledge*</u> *of God the Father, through sanctification of the Spirit, unto obedience and sprinkling of the blood of Jesus Christ: Grace unto you, and peace, be multiplied.* Foreknowledge means to know beforehand. Foreknowledge comes from the Greek word *prognosis*. It is familiar to us because of the medical profession. Doctors can make a prognosis and determine <u>beforehand</u> the life or death of a patient. Because of their foreknowledge, they can do that.

God, in His foreknowledge, knew beforehand who

217

would receive Jesus Christ and who would reject Him, and He chose the ones who would believe and surrender their lives to Him as the elect. He chose them because He knew them before the world was created. That's how awesome our God is.

Blinded Eyes And Hardened Hearts

The subject of who could or could not believe would not be complete without understanding this prophecy fulfilled in John 12. People hardened their hearts against God because they were unwilling to submit to His authority. It started with Satan and those who love the miracle power he gave to defy God's will and do evil. He did the same to Jesus during His 40 days in the wilderness. Instead of Israel calling Jesus the Son of God, they called Him a devil. Jesus told the Jews in John chapter 8 that their father was the devil. Perhaps the most fitting verse with insight into why God blinds and hardens the hearts of those who reject Him is in Galatians 6:7, *Be not deceived; God is not mocked: for whatsoever a man soweth, that shall he also reap.* The application is if you harden your heart in defiance of

God's will, look out for you may reap the same and more than you could imagine. Pharaoh should have been a warning example to Israel: Exodus 8:15, *But when <u>Pharaoh</u> saw that there was respite* [relief]*, he <u>hardened his heart</u>, and hearkened not unto them; as the LORD had said.* The LORD knew (foreknowledge) that both Pharaoh and Isreal would rebel because they were the serpent's seed. Israel's hatred for God's authority is why they sought to kill Jesus, not because they were predestinated to damnation by sovereign salvation.

John 12:36, *While ye have light, believe in the light, that ye may be the children of light. These things spake Jesus, and departed, and did hide himself from them. 37 <u>But though he had done so many miracles</u> before them, <u>yet they believed not on him</u>: 38 That the saying of Esaias the prophet might be fulfilled, which he spake, Lord, who hath believed our report? and to whom hath the arm of the Lord been revealed? 39 Therefore they could not believe, because that Esaias said again, 40 He hath blinded their eyes, and* *hardened their heart; that they should not see with their eyes, nor understand with their heart, and be converted, and I should heal them. 41 These things said Esaias, when he saw his glory, and spake of him. 42 Nevertheless among the chief rulers also many believed on him; but because of the Pharisees they did not confess him, lest they should be put out of the synagogue: 43* <u>*For they loved the praise of men more than the praise of God*</u> [Jesus knew the thoughts of their hearts] *44 Jesus cried and said, He that believeth on me, believeth not on me, but on him that sent me. 45 And he that seeth me seeth him that sent me. 46 I am come a light into the world, that* <u>*whosoever believeth on me*</u> *should not abide in darkness.* For the last time, Jesus makes His appeal to the people to believe in Him and not harden their hearts. Some would do that, and Nicodemus was one of them.

Adoption

In the early Jewish tradition, adoption <u>was not</u> a ceremony for adding a new child to a family. It was a formal announcement for a son reaching 13 or 14 years old and then the heir to his father's inheritance. He was not becoming a family member, for he was already a son in the family. <u>Jewish adoption was not relational; it was positional.</u> Adoption for a Christian is the immediate position as joint-heirs with Christ when he is born of the Spirit and becomes a child of God: Romans 8:14, *For <u>as many as are led by the Spirit of God, they are the sons of God</u>. 15 For ye have not received the spirit of bondage again to fear; but ye have received the Spirit of adoption, whereby we cry, Abba, Father. 16 The Spirit itself beareth witness with our spirit, that we are the children of God: 17 <u>And if children</u>, then <u>heirs</u>; <u>heirs of God</u>, <u>and joint-heirs with Christ</u>; if so be that we <u>suffer with him</u>, that <u>we may be also glorified together</u>.*

The Holy Spirit indwells and leads the new Christian in being made again into the image of Christ. It is a lifelong process of sanctification in becoming more like Jesus Christ. Sanctification is complete at glorification in a resurrected body like Jesus' resurrected, glorified Body. What a day that will be!

WORKS SALVATION

Not by works of righteousness which we have done, but according to his mercy he saved us, by the washing of regeneration, and renewing of the Holy Ghost (Titus 3:5).

It might be an excellent place to let the Scriptures show us the meaning of salvation and then go from there. *Not by works of righteousness* means sinners cannot do things to merit or earn God's forgiveness for breaking His laws. These words take us right back to Genesis 2 and 3. It is not a person's works that save; Christ's work saves us. What did He do so we could be forgiven of our sins? Jesus was pictured as the Sacrifice in Genesis chapter 3. He suffered in our place and for the sins of all people, making it possible for their salvation. What is salvation? It is the deliverance from eternal death and the possession of eternal life with Jesus Christ in His kingdom that begins in Revelation 21. *But according to his mercy he saved us.* Mercy means loving-kindness. Mankind is set apart from all creation because God created Adam and Eve in His image and likeness. Adam and Eve did not rebel against God. The serpent deceived Eve with a lie. Disobeying God because of deception is different than disobeying Him because of knowingly and willing refusing to obey Him.

The Rules

Nevertheless, Adam and Eve sinned. When Eve was tempted to doubt God's Word, she should have trusted Him. The context and harmony rules that Jesus taught His disciples would help us to test any doctrine to determine if it is true or false, right or wrong. Without the rules, one can make the Bible appear to say something totally different from what God says: *And the serpent said unto the woman, Ye shall not surely die.* What the serpent said is both contextually and harmoniously contradictory to what God said in Genesis 2:17: *But of the tree of the knowledge of good and evil, thou shalt not eat of it: for in the day that thou eatest thereof thou shalt surely die.*

How does God save sinners? He saves them by a new

birth: *washing regeneration and renewing the Holy Ghost.* God's command is for all sinners to believe in His Son, Jesus Christ, and surrender (to yield, something they do willingly) their lives to Him. When a sinner does that, the Holy Spirit will make him a child of God. Jesus taught that to Nicodemus in John chapter 3. It is called being born again or born from above, that is born of God.

Works salvation and sovereign salvation are the product of false doctrine that contradicts many Scripture verses. If it only disagreed with one, it would still be wrong. Titus 3:5 says it's *Not by works of righteousness which we have done, but according to his mercy he saved us, by the washing of regeneration, and renewing of the Holy Ghost.* And Matthew 11:28, *Come unto me, all ye that labour and are heavy laden, and I will give you rest.* Now that should be enough truth for anyone who wants the truth.

ARE YOU A CHILD OF GOD?

The Spirit itself beareth witness with our spirit, that we are the children of God (Romans 8:16).

Imagine how horrible it would be to live your life thinking you are one of God's children headed for His kingdom, and you were mistaken. Romans 8, to a large extent, is talking about the Holy Spirit's presence in the believer. The lingering question is this: Are these believers professors or possessors of Christ and salvation? A few key questions will help you find your context in the reality of being born of the Spirit and led by Him.

Some things to think about are:

1. Do you have a love for God's Word? It's the key to learning how to love Him and walk with Him each day of your life.
2. Do you confess your sins the moment you are convicted and then keep asking the Lord for victory?
3. Do you talk with the Lord all the time? I mean,

as David did in the Psalms? He had a real relationship with his wonderful Savior. So should all of God's children.

4. Do you have a desire to know God's will for your life so you can serve Him with the talents He has given you?
5. Or do you feel salvation was something forced upon you and are not deeply interested in being close to your Heavenly Father?

Jesus said that loving obedience is what makes the relationship with God a reality. Look what He said in John 14:22-24, *Judas saith unto him, not Iscariot, Lord, how is it that thou wilt manifest thyself unto us, and not unto the world? 23 Jesus answered and said unto him, If a man love me, he will keep my words: and my Father will love him, and we will come unto him, and make our abode with him. 24 He that loveth me not keepeth not my sayings ....*

How can a child of God experience His abode? The Apostle John answers this question, and you will find it by reading the gospel that bears his name.

JESUS' PARTING DAYS

Jesus said, I am the resurrection, and the life: he that believeth in me, though he were dead, yet shall he live: And whosoever liveth and believeth in me shall never die. Believest thou this (John 11:25-26)?

The final days Jesus spent with the disciples were full of disappointment and sorrow that quickly turned into joy and victory. Jesus spent His last days near Bethany. Jerusalem is a short walk of about two miles westward. It was Bethany beyond Jordan where Jesus was baptized by John the Baptist and where His ministry began. John chapter 12 begins by saying; *Six days before the Passover*. Jesus knew it was His time to be glorified. He would be the Passover Lamb pictured from Genesis to Exodus to Calvary.

The raising of Lazarus and Jesus' interactions with Martha and Mary gives us a glimpse of our Savior's personal and loving relationships with those who loved Him. What they experienced is possible for any child of God. Our God is not a respecter of persons, but He knows those who love and respect Him. What Jesus said in John 14:22-23 is meant for us also: *Judas saith unto him, not Iscariot, Lord, how is it that thou wilt manifest thyself unto us, and not unto the world? 23 Jesus answered and said unto him,* <u>*If a man love me, he will keep my words*</u>*: and my Father will love him, and* <u>*we will come unto him, and make our abode with him*</u>*.*

After the Lord's supper, He and the eleven disciples go to the Garden of Gethsemane to pray. It is very near the Mount of Olives. The Mount of Olives is a hill east of Jerusalem. The Garden of Gethsemane is a short way down this small hill toward the Old City of Jerusalem. These places mark the footsteps of Jesus until His ascension.

Mary's anointing of Jesus begins His time of preparing His disciples for the disappointing and heartbreaking events that are soon to come. May the chapter titles from John 12-21 help us remember these precious moments.

Greeks Seek Jesus

In John chapter 12, the announcement of the Greeks seeking Jesus seems to be a signal of His glorification. Jesus called Calvary and His resurrection His glorification. Jesus had just made His glorious entrance into Jerusalem with the people spreading palm branches in the way and crying, *"Hosanna: Blessed is the King of Israel."*

Shortly after this, disciples came to Him with this message: John 12:20-23, *And there were certain Greeks among them that came up to worship at the feast: 21 The same came therefore to Philip, which was of Bethsaida of Galilee, and desired him, saying, Sir, we would see Jesus. 22 Philip cometh and telleth Andrew: and again Andrew and Philip tell Jesus. 23 And Jesus answered them, saying,* <u>*The hour is come, that the Son of man should be glorified*</u>.

Washing Of The Feet

In John chapter 13, Jesus teaches us all the lessons of humility and servitude: John 13:13-17, *Ye call me Master and Lord: and ye say well; for so I am. 14 If I then, your Lord and Master, have washed your feet; ye also ought to wash one another's feet. 15 For I have given you an example, that ye should do as I have done to you. 16 Verily, verily, I say unto you, The servant is not greater than his lord; neither he that is sent greater than he that sent him. 17 If ye know these things, happy are ye if ye do them.*

Many Mansions

In John chapter 14, Jesus speaks of His Father's house, the temple, His dwelling place. Later, He gives the Apostle John a preview of the New Earth and the Holy City, the eternal home of God's children in the kingdom of righteousness in Revelation 21.

Vine And Branches

In John chapter 15, Jesus uses "abide" many times to emphasize the fundamental nature of the Christian's life. If you don't depend on Christ, you can do nothing. Without relying on Him, your prayers will not be answered. If you are not fruitful, you belong with the branches that will be burned. Judas Iscariot is identified with all of these negative characteristics.

Here are a few of the "abides" in John 15:2, *Every branch in me that beareth not fruit he taketh away: and every branch that beareth fruit, he purgeth it, that it may bring forth more fruit; 4 Abide in me, and I in you. As the branch cannot bear fruit of itself, except it abide in the vine; no more can ye, except ye abide in me; 6 If a man abide not in me, he is cast forth as a branch, and is withered; and men gather them, and cast them into the fire, and they are burned; 7 If ye abide in me, and my words abide in you, ye shall ask what ye will, and it shall be done unto you.*

The Holy Spirit

In John chapter 16, Jesus teaches us about the Comforter, the Holy Spirit. The Comforter is God, Christ in us; the hope of glory: John 16:7-11;33, *Nevertheless I tell you the truth; It is expedient for you that I go away: for if I go not away, the Comforter will not come unto you; but if I depart, I will send him unto you. 8 And when he is come, he will reprove the world of sin, and of righteousness, and of judgment: 9 Of sin, because they believe not on me; 10 Of righteousness, because I go to my Father, and ye see me no more; 11 Of judgment, because the prince of this world is judged; 33 These things I have spoken unto you, that in me ye might have peace. In the world ye shall have tribulation: but be of good cheer; I have overcome the world.*

Lovest Thou Me?

In John 21, Jesus comes to Peter and asks him three times if he loved Him. The Lord said to Peter, "*Lovest Me more than these?*" Now, the Lord knew who *these* would be some years later. The Apostle Paul found Peter compromising the gospel by turning away from the gentile Christians to keep his standing with those who mixed the law and grace in Galatians 2:11-13, *But when Peter was come to Antioch, I withstood him* [Peter] *to the face, because he was to be blamed. 12 For before that certain came from James, he did eat with the Gentiles: but when they were come, he withdrew and separated himself, fearing them which were of the circumcision. 13 And the other Jews dissembled likewise with him; insomuch that Barnabas also was carried away with their dissimulation* [hyprocisy].

The Kingdom of Israel

The greatest concern of the disciples, before Jesus left, was the kingdom of Israel. All the preaching Jesus did about the kingdom of God seemed to have gone over their heads. Their question was bypassed. Building the church is the Lord's priority. Witnessing in the power of the Holy Spirit is how the gospel will impact the world. Jesus gave them their last instructions in Acts 1:6-9, *When they therefore were come together, they asked of him, saying, Lord, wilt thou at this time restore again the kingdom to Israel? 7 And he said unto them, It is not for you to know the times or the seasons, which the Father hath put in his own power. 8 But ye shall receive power, after that the Holy Ghost is come upon you: and ye shall be witnesses unto me both in Jerusalem, and in all Judaea, and in Samaria, and unto the uttermost part of the earth. 9 And when he had spoken these things, while they beheld, he was taken up; and a cloud received him out of their sight.*

The Kingdom Of God

Heaven and beyond is the reality of every saint's hope. To be absent from the body is to be present with the Lord, now in the third heaven where Jesus is. Is that where the children of God will spend eternity? If you were thinking yes, then look beyond to the kingdom of God. It begins when His earth is destroyed: Heaven and beyond is the reality of every saint's hope.

Isaiah 51:6

Lift up your eyes to the heavens, and look upon the earth beneath: for the heavens shall vanish away like smoke, and the earth shall wax old like a garment, and they that dwell therein shall die in like manner: but my salvation shall be for ever, and my righteousness shall not be abolished.

Matthew 24:35

Jesus said, *Heaven and earth shall pass away, but my words shall not pass away.*

2 Peter 3:10-13

But the day of the Lord will come as a thief in the night; in the which the heavens shall pass away with a great noise, and the elements shall melt with fervent heat, the earth also and the works that are therein shall be burned up. 11 Seeing then that all these things shall be dissolved, what manner of persons ought ye to be in all holy conversation and godliness, 12 Looking for and hasting unto the coming of the day of God, wherein the heavens being on fire shall be dissolved, and the elements shall melt with fervent heat? 13 Nevertheless we, according to his promise, look for new heavens and a new earth, wherein dwelleth righteousness.

Then Christ's eternal kingdom of righteousness begins.

Revelation 21:1-5

And I saw a new heaven and a new earth: for the first heaven and the first earth were passed away; and there was no more sea. 2 And I John saw the holy city, new Jerusalem, coming down from God out of heaven, prepared as a bride adorned for her husband. 3 And I heard a great voice out of heaven saying, Behold, the tabernacle of God is with men, and he will dwell with them, and they shall be his people, and God himself shall be with them, and be their God. 4 And God shall wipe away all tears from their eyes; and there shall be no more death, neither sorrow, nor crying, neither shall there be any more pain: for the former things are passed away. 5 And he that sat upon the throne said, Behold, I make all things new. And he said unto me, Write: for these words are true and faithful.

What does it mean to be a child of God? To me, it is the greatest gift ever given. Revelation 21:3 brings tears to my eyes. To think of Jesus saying He will dwell with us and we shall be His people, and He will be our God. Then He wipes away all our tears, says there will be no more death, sorrow, crying, or pain, for they are passed away, and all things become new. Dear brothers and sisters in Christ, it will be worth it all.

Jesus said, *The kingdom of heaven is like unto treasure hid in a field; the which when a man hath found, he hideth, and for joy thereof goeth and selleth all that he hath, and buyeth that field. Again, the kingdom of heaven is like unto a merchant man, seeking goodly pearls: Who, when he had found one pearl of great price, went and sold all that he had, and bought it.*

www.ingramcontent.com/pod-product-compliance
Lightning Source LLC
Chambersburg PA
CBHW060822050426
42453CB00008B/549